Art Works!

W9-BLN-307

Also Available in the Moving Middle Schools Series

More Than the Truth
Teaching Nonfiction Writing Through Journalism

Through Mathematical Eyes
Exploring Functional Relationships in Math and Science

Digging Deep
Teaching Social Studies Through the Study of Archaeology

Art Works!

Interdisciplinary Learning Powered by the Arts

Edited by
**Dennie Palmer Wolf
and Dana Balick**

DISCARDED
JENKS LRC
GORDON COLLEGF

JENKS LIBRARY
GORDON COLLEGE
255 GRAPEVINE RD.
WENHAM, MA 01984

HEINEMANN
Portsmouth, NH

Heinemann
A division of Reed Elsevier Inc.
361 Hanover Street
Portsmouth, NH 03801-3912
http://www.heinemann.com

Offices and agents throughout the world

© 1999 by Heinemann

All rights reserved. No part of this book may be reproduced in any form or by any electronic or mechanical means, including information storage and retrieval systems, without permission in writing from the publisher, except by a reviewer, who may quote brief passages in a review.

The author and publisher wish to thank those who have generously given permission to reprint borrowed material.

CIP is on file with the Library of Congress.
ISBN: 0-325-00116-2

Consulting editor: Maureen Barbieri
Production: Vicki Kasabian
Cover illustration: Bronwyn Uber
Cover design: Jenny Jensen Greenleaf
Manufacturing: Louise Richardson

Printed in the United States of America on acid-free paper
02 01 00 99 98 ML 1 2 3 4 5

Contents

Preface: A Word About This Series

Beginning in 1991 with a grant from the Rockefeller Foundation, PACE, an unusual collaborative of urban educators, got underway. In six sites across the country (Fort Worth, Texas; Pittsburgh, Pennsylvania; Rochester, New York; San Diego and San Francisco, California; and Wilmington, Delaware), teams of teachers began creating "portfolio cultures"—classrooms that emphasized growth toward high common standards. The image of a classroom as a culture where a complex network of daily actions supported thinking and imagination provided an important tool for rethinking not just assessment, but curriculum, teaching, and connections to families and surrounding communities.

It was no accident that this work was centered in middle schools. Early adolescence is one of the most promising and most vulnerable moments in the life span of young Americans. Contrary to our stereotypical views of adolescents, many students between the ages of ten and fifteen have their eyes intensely focused on the world "out there." They want to know "What kind of place is there for me—and others like me?" When the answer is harsh and discouraging, we see cynicism, doubt, and disengagement. When the answer is honest and makes a place for young people to invest in modern urban life, we get back energy and work, along with invention and insight.

Early in our work of creating portfolio cultures, we began to question the usual proposition that "as soon as schools are orderly, safe, and respectful, we will be able to launch new kinds of learning." Absolutely true, in one sense: neither teachers nor students can learn in danger. But one day, as we looked at the costs of installing metal detectors in all of one city's middle schools, a teacher and a central office administrator brought a question to the larger group: "Couldn't it be that once learning is underway, then we will see more orderly, safer, and respectful schools?" In the wake of that startling reversal, we began to think about the major learning challenges that young adolescents could take on and enjoy—which could make it possible for many more of them to travel from elementary to high school thinking of themselves as authors, scientists, historians, artists, and mathematicians.

In that process, we developed a unique way of working together that we have come to call "curriculum seminars." The seminars are a series of professional development experiences geared to support teachers in developing materials and approaches to teach important content, powerful strategies, and big ideas. We didn't identify those challenges overnight. After spending almost two years in middle schools across the nation, we knew it to be a world of almost wild contrasts. In some settings, students wrote, did research, and investigated mathematical regularities in the natural world. Elsewhere the curriculum was at a stagnant level; as one student commented, "I did the work of a third grader for three years." We also knew that in some middle schools valuable time was spent on gimmicks: math "problems of the week" that involved endless calculations and little thinking, word searches for science vocabulary, models of the universe made from gumdrops, or computer games masquerading as historical simulations.

We knew that middle school was three years that most students—especially those in city schools—did not have to waste. Working in the strongest middle schools in the six sites that we had chosen, we began a series of interviews in which we asked experienced middle school teachers to think out loud about the major learning tasks of middle school. What we were looking for had two characteristics. First, we wanted what one teacher called "the rod and the staff" or "the sword and buckler" of learning and what another suggested was the equivalent of the microscope or movable type: "Small revolutions of the mind and heart."

Second, these valued performances (as we began to call them) encapsulated understandings that were challenging to teach, especially to students who "didn't either arrive already knowing them, or at least being close to it." And if we were out-and-out blunt, we would admit that schools rarely managed to confer these capacities on the students who depended on school the most—those whose families and life circumstances could not supply these understandings.

In addition to our interviews, we asked teachers to look at collections of student work from their own and other sites to identify evidence of these understandings—or the lack thereof. We also observed in classes and spoke to high school teachers. As we collected nominations, the consensus was almost unanimous within and strong across disciplines. Once we boiled it down, the list was short. Teachers wanted to work together on enabling their students to:

- write powerful nonfiction
- bridge the concrete work of arithmetic to the conceptual and formal world of mathematics that permits modeling and prediction
- use multiple sources (especially primary sources) as evidence to piece together a larger whole, such as an hypothesis and research, an investigation, or an argument
- create an original work (for instance, a series of poems, a story, a theatrical or musical performance) with some grace and humanity, polished through consulting others and revision.

Fine, but then what? The first step was to search for settings or enterprises where these performances and understandings are practiced in "real life" so we could study them in "their natural habitat." Many twists and turns later, we came up with:

- journalism
- science investigations that employed mathematics to capture regularities
- archaeological research
- the collaborative work of companies of artists such as those who work on operas, museum exhibitions, or new editions of classic novels.

With these working models in mind, we asked teachers in the PACE network if they would become involved in a two-year process in which they would develop curriculum using these enterprises as models. These became our curriculum seminars in which teachers, researchers, and outside experts:

- used portfolios of work from both struggling and accomplished students to investigate what prevents large numbers of students from being successful at gaining major understandings
- took on the role of novice learners in immersion experiences that took us deep into the workrooms and thoughts of adults whose life-

work depends on these understandings (journalists, scientists, archaeologists, musicians, and artists). This took us to the city to write journalism, into a collaboration with scientists and mathematicians, to a museum to look at the artifacts of Mayan civilization, and ultimately into settings where artists collaborated

- designed and drafted curricula to make these big ideas and powerful strategies available to students
- taught the curricula and brought the evidence of student work back to the seminar for help, information, and critique
- revised and retaught the curricula
- thought about the resulting student work in the light of demanding performance standards
- reflected on what we had learned
- presented and published what we knew from our work together.

In this last step, teachers once again stepped outside of their classrooms. This time they became authors. In this phase of our work, we were often joined by other teachers who were doing similar work in their schools and classrooms. Two things emerged. First, the chapters in this book describe what is possible for young adolescent learners—no matter what their history, income, country of origin, or first language. Second, the book contains a new vision of accomplished teachers' work. The teachers whose stories you will read insisted that this kind of hybrid between intense classroom engagement and adult reflection was something they never again wanted to be without.

But, as any reader knows, the genuine "last" step of any work doesn't belong to the authors. It belongs to readers—those who put it to use. You and your colleagues (be they fellow teachers or students) will read and reflect, implement and revise what you find between these covers. So be it.

Acknowledgments

This series, Moving Middle Schools, is the result of many people joining together and buckling down. We want to begin by thanking the author-teachers who were willing to venture into what was to be a mix of teaching, researching, writing, and collegial exchange. They signed up without a recipe, participated in seminars with strangers, taught using unforeseen methods, and reflected on their work by writing after school and into the nights. Behind the teachers are the colleagues and principals who covered classes, read drafts, and made exceptions. Behind those educators are the urban districts that worked with us to endorse serious school reform: Fort Worth, Texas; Pittsburgh, Pennsylvania; Rochester, New York; San Diego and San Francisco, California; and Wilmington, Delaware. We also want to thank the students who made these projects possible. They gave generously of their time, their thoughts, and their writing. They, too, were without a blueprint. Just back of the students are families who stayed up to proofread, went to the library one more time, attended field trips, or answered interview questions when they could have gone out, read, napped, or eaten supper.

We also owe thanks to another set of "critical friends"—people who worked along with us, even as they asked difficult questions and set high standards: Edmund Gordon, Carol Bonilla-Bowman, Melissa Lemons, and Patty Taylor. We also want to thank the many educators from institutions outside of school who have helped us: Shelly Bransford, Greg Jenkins, Robin Jensen, and Lynne Williamson. Most recently, we are indebted to the editors and staff of Heinemann who were willing to work with us, even though we were, and remain, a collaborative, with all the varied ideas and voices that term implies.

Finally, we want to thank those who, as many as seven years ago, were willing to support research on school reform in urban settings. This work grew to become PACE (Performance Assessment

Collaboratives for Education), a network of urban school districts committed to high standards of practice for students, teachers, and schools that historically have not experienced sustained support and abundant resources. PACE invented the curriculum seminars that, in turn, gave birth to this series of books. That original generosity—in particular, the willingness to provide a rare several years of work together—has made us remember that the first meaning of the word *foundation* is a solid footing on which a structure can be built. So we thank Alberta Arthurs, Hugh Price, Jamie Jensen, and Marla Ucelli at the Rockefeller Foundation; Warren Simmons and Lynn White at the Annie E. Casey Foundation; and Jane Polin at the GE Fund.

Introduction

The Fine Art of Being a Park Ranger:
Or Why Thickness, Wellsprings,
and Company Matter

Dennie Palmer Wolf

If you were to read his job description, it might call for a knowledge of boating and tides, maybe even the ability to swim or to disperse unruly crowds. Chances are, it would never mention landscape design or theatre. However, if you listen to John Nove, a park ranger on the Boston Harbor Islands, the ways of knowing we associate with the arts play a surprisingly powerful role in energizing and amplifying his understanding of the thirty small land masses he already knows like the back of his hand. For instance, as you listen to him talk about his work you realize that he thinks about the islands as studios for learning how to see:

> As a naturalist, I think about the difference between looking and seeing. Everyone climbs out of the water taxi and looks around. But not too many of them know how to see what's here: the wind, the tide, the effects of the seasons. So I've taken that on as a challenge. I've put a pole on the dock to dramatize how rapidly the water level changes with the tide. I'm cultivating wildflowers, like chickory and jimsonweed, that open and close at different times of day to make the passage of time and the effects of light visible.

He also thinks of the islands not just as acres, but as theatres:

> I've been watching a history student who was working on one of the islands. He developed a character, the postmaster of the

1

Confederacy, who was imprisoned on one of the Harbor islands during the Civil War. Even in August, he'd dress in character, complete with wool underwear. He would read this man's journal and his letters home so he could give a tour as a Southerner, a man who was bitter about being penned up in an island prison as a war criminal. He could even make ironic comments about how the richer prisoners had their meals catered from Boston restaurants.

People, even kids, were really drawn in by him. And it sent me hunting around for a character. I think I've come up with one who is actually a lot like me. He's Alvin Sweeney, Physician-in-Chief of the quarantine hospital on one of the islands in the twenties and thirties. He was a driven horticulturalist. All the fruit trees, the lilacs, the dogwoods, even exotic plants like the tamarisk tree are his handiwork. So I'm thinking of maybe becoming Alvin Sweeney next summer.

Quirky? The teachers and researchers who have brought this book together would say, "Absolutely not." Even though few of them are artists by training, they have all witnessed how the ways of thinking and working that are characteristic of the arts spark appetite, affection, imagination, attention, and a near fever for quality in their students. Far from just being awed, these teachers have thought long and hard about how the arts power learning. Their trio of hunches includes: thickness, wellsprings, and company.

Thickness

The anthropologist Clifford Geertz has long argued that to understand a culture other than our own, we need "thick description," nuanced and empathetic accounts of life elsewhere, not head counts, lists of holidays, or the names of rituals. Without even being asked, John's stories underscore the remarkable power of the arts to promote a similar kind of "textured" understanding. When John describes his careful placement of a tide pole and his plans for seeding the island meadows with light-sensitive wildflowers, he does two things at once. He reminds us of the difference between ordinary looking and seeing. And he takes huge personal pleasure in imagining, inventing, and implementing ways that will make the ecology of the harbor islands visible. He is inventing a world that is thick with meaning—and enjoying it.

Separately and together, all of the authors in this volume echo John. They use the arts to ensure that their students acquire a taste for this same kind of thick understanding. In Chapter 1, Julie Craven and Lynn Brown insist that their students understand the cultures of the Middle East through the lens of architecture. They want their students to capture the long-running confluences and conflicts of the region using domes, arches, minarets, brick, and stone. The point is to learn—through mind and hand and eye—how architecture both embodies and shapes a cultural environment. In her chapter, Karen Sorin describes how students at the New School do much more than read about the Harlem Renaissance. They build their understanding by performing the literature, dances, and songs of those years. In learning the Charleston or "The Negro Speaks of Rivers," students have to acquire not just names and dates, but the rhythms and cadences that Bessie Smith and Langston Hughes insisted were the new voice of America.

Wellsprings

John Nove's ability to make the distinction between looking and seeing is critical to his work as a naturalist and as a ranger. His view of the islands as studios and theatres embodies another way in which the arts can ignite learning. The arts teach skills like visual thinking, acute listening, and a sensitivity to metaphor that are wellsprings—feeding and informing all kinds of understanding. These wellspring skills are doubly powerful. They give students sharp-edged tools they can apply outside the studio or off the stage, but they also signal that learning is not a series of distinct classes and topics, but an integrated enterprise.

Many of the writers in this volume touch on these wellspring skills. Craven and Brown want their students to be able to read the face of buildings just as closely as they examine the prayers of Christian, Jewish, and Moslem believers. Sorin wants her students to be able to hear jazz and poetry. But the power of these wellspring skills is absolutely at the center of Lue Stilley's chapter on visual thinking. As they apply keen observation to science, history, and archaeology, Stilley's students show us the pleasure and energy students experience as they learn not only to notice details, but to see patterns.

Companies of Learners

In the acknowledgments to her novel, *The Shipping News,* Annie Proulx thanks writers and editors she has known. But she also thanks naturalists and seamen:

> Help came in many directions in the writing of *The Shipping News.* . . . Canadian Coast Guard Search and Rescue Personnel, the staff of the *Northern Pen* in St. Anthony, fishermen and loggers, the Atmospheric Environment Service of Environment Canada all told me how things worked . . . Walter Punch of the Massachusetts Horticultural Society Library confirmed some obscure horticultural references. (Proulx 1993)

Although the Newfoundland world she creates is largely a product of her own imagination, Proulx knows she would never have understood the storm systems, the birds, and the plants of Newfoundland unless she had had company. John's story of bumping into an historian's view of the islands makes a similar point. Together, the writer and the ranger remind us that the arts excite because they are profoundly social—but in a very particular way. Collaboration in the arts is energizing, not because the labor is shared, but because the labor is divided.

Many artworks, whether they are illustrated books or theatre productions, get their quality and energy because they bring together quite different talents and disparate points of view. Bill Amorosi and Susan Barahal explore this in their chapter where they describe the work of teams of young writers and illustrators bringing out a new edition of *The Hobbit.* David Dik makes exactly this point in his chapter where he explores the energies behind what occurs in opera companies. There a composer, librettist, musicians, set designers, costumers, and stage managers all make their distinctive contributions to a production.

In these projects, work is structured so that every role has to contribute high-quality work for the project to emerge as strong and interesting. Singers can only do so much for poor music, and a composer needs singers who will give life and verve to his or her music. An author's work can be dulled by ho-hum illustrations that only depict, rather than enhance, the story line. In both cases, the total is a tight mosaic of separate parts. In closing the volume, Dana Balick insists that teachers deserve this same kind of company. If we want classrooms where the arts are an integral part of learning, then teachers need time with writers, stage directors, artists, and curators.

But none of the teachers or researchers writing here would claim that creating textured understanding, feeding wellspring skills, or creating a company of learners occurs quickly or assuredly. At one time or another, all of them have encountered (or been caught up in) projects where the arts were shoehorned into some unnatural or trivial union: a project about ancient Greece where the art was a colored pencil sketch of a fifth-century vase or an illustrated time line. And although these author-teachers don't necessarily identify themselves as artists, actors, or musicians, they aren't interested in having students trace over a photo, make a diorama, or write a rap about the order of the planets. If the arts are coming to their classrooms, these teachers want the very best. And this volume is the story of how they got it.

Beginning from the End

The Jerusalem Architecture Project

Lynn Brown and Julie Craven

A group of visiting educators walked into our Humanities classrooms one Friday at the end of May. We had been expecting them, and the students barely turned their heads. They were too engaged in the urgency of their tasks to pay these adults much attention. In three days, students were going to present their Jerusalem projects in an exhibition for the school community. The projects were the culmination of a unit on the Middle East. Their task: to design a public facility that built community across the city's diverse populations and was, at the same time, true to Jerusalem's past, present, and future. A completed project included an architectural sketch (with at least two perspectives), a scale model, and an essay explaining how the building met the project goals. On the day the visitors walked into the classroom, the students had already been engaged in the creative process for weeks. And, with the exhibition fast approaching, they were on a mission. Walls needed to be squared up, domes covered, mosaics drawn, writing polished, and facts checked. The students were, of course, polite to the visitors. Who doesn't love an appreciative audience? So as they scored foam core with their X-Acto knives, they pointed out where their buildings incorporated Muslim, Christian, and Jewish symbols or one historical period from which an architectural feature was drawn. Writers made use of the visitors for feedback on next-to-final drafts. If their point was clear to a visitor, it surely would be to their upcoming audience. Mostly, students worked and visitors watched.

As the period drew to a close, the visitors had questions for us, the teachers. How did we learn to teach like this? Where did we get the idea for this project?

We still laugh at those questions. Just what kind of teaching did they see? On that particular day, our "teaching" involved holding a wall while someone glued it, or directing a student to an unused T-square. We probably picked up a few scraps and pushed in a few chairs, too. We also knew that if these visitors had come a few days earlier, they would have seen a very different scene. We would have been removing yard-sticks from the hands of ninja warriors and threatening to end the project all together if students didn't get serious. Our consciences were also twinging. We were all too aware of the glaring holes in the content we had asked our students to study and the limits of the processes we had them use. Moreover, we had questions about the level of truthfulness and respect with which we had asked our students to explore a subject that involves people struggling and suffering in a terrible, ongoing conflict. The visitors' arrival happened to be one of those happy coincidences—they came when the project had acquired a life of its own.

Yet the visitors' questions have stuck with us. How do we figure out how to teach a particular subject? How do we decide how to structure a unit or design a project? What role does our school's structure play? Why does interdisciplinary work have such a major role in our decisions? This chapter is our attempt to answer these questions, for ourselves as much as for anyone. In the act of answering, we hope to help ourselves fill the gaps and see the missed opportunities.

The Role of School Structure

Our school structure and philosophy are important elements of our decision-making process. The Martin Luther King Jr. Open School is a K–8 public school in Cambridge, Massachusetts, with a diverse student body of approximately 360. The school community believes that student learning improves with greater opportunity for developmental growth. Therefore, after kindergarten, students are grouped in cross-grade classrooms: 1/2, 3/4, 5/6, and 7/8. They have the same teacher for two years; each year half the class moves on and a new group enters. This allows for more continuity between grade levels with students at each learning level alternating between being newcomers and experienced learners. At the 7/8 level, while there are separate Math and Science classes, in Humanities (integrated Language Arts and Social Studies) students are again mixed cross-grade and the curriculum is on a two-year cycle. Humanities classes are double periods ranging from one-and-a-half- to two-hour blocks. Our schedule also gives us team meeting times and common prep periods so the entire 7/8 team is constantly communicating about students, schedule, and curriculum. Thus, our very structure enables integration and facilitates project work.

"We" are the Humanities teachers. We work as we wrote this chapter, planning and reflecting together so that on most days, the agendas and homework in our two classrooms look identical. We are fortunate to have found each other. We both value collaboration and honestly feel that our curriculum planned together is more rigorous and has greater integrity than anything that we could do individually. What we do would be much harder if we were alone, at a more traditional school. This chapter is as much a result of our collaboration as is the project it features.

Our View of Interdisciplinary Teaching

Our goal is to create a classroom environment in which students have opportunities to work and learn in the ways that excite us when we work and learn; the best vehicle we have found for producing this environment is interdisciplinary teaching. In our experience, the power of an interdisciplinary approach is that it approximates how people learn, a prerequisite if any of what we teach is to stick with our students. We don't learn in self-contained episodes with clearly identified teachers. Our knowledge is a montage of information gathered from our families, our lovers, our friends and colleagues, and our experiences. For example, what we know about democracy may begin with memories of family political affiliations and discussions (or lack of them), mixed with our own voting history, what we learned in our grade-school civics classes, and tempered by our personal collisions with social and economic inequality. We may redefine those ideas as we watch news reports on the retreat of Soviet-style communism or on the veiled campaign donations of multinational corporations. We might have been struck enough at some point to do some extra research or pose more pointed questions to friends about their impressions of the meaning of democracy. Our journey is serpentine and serendipitous, fed by chance meetings, directed interests or intentional avoidances, and resources. As knowledge increases, so can the purposefulness of the journey. We often choose to learn more because we want to and because we can. At these times, we are driven by the surprising realization that we know enough to ask more and better questions.

We know that school structures—mandated content, predetermined schedules, competing demands for attention—limit the degree to which this kind of learning can unfold for students. Yet we believe that cross-disciplinary teaching maximizes opportunities for students to engage in satisfying learning journeys within these confines. It provides for a 360-degree view of a topic along with a multitude of entry points for students. Such variety increases our chances of engaging students enough for them to want to learn more—the one who finds politics off-putting may find the idea of designing her own building irresistible, and vice-versa.

So, how can we ensure that interdisciplinary learning occurs? When we plan an interdisciplinary unit, we start with three basic questions:

- What is important for us to teach?
- How are we going to teach this in a way that engages our students and ourselves?
- What will support what and how we want to teach?

Our first planning question is the most difficult. Teachers must always decide what to include and what to leave out. In the spring of 1997, we were supposed to teach The Middle East. In our case, everything about the Middle East. But how could we include the breadth of what is important (and mandated), while getting at the part of learning that is engaging and fun and more in-depth?

Our potential answers and ideas form around our second question: How do we engage students and ourselves? What is a project that will satisfy us as teachers and our students as learners? This culminating project needs to demand real understanding and knowledge and needs to appeal to seventh and eighth graders' innate curiosity and love of fun. Envisioning the project at the end of our unit before we begin to plan gives us a framework for deciding what to include and what to leave out. Our focus has to become the knowledge and skills our students need to do this project well. Moreover, when we introduce a project early on, its existence as a distant vision sets a context for what students learn. They start the creative process almost immediately; and with the act of creating comes a desire—at times a demand—to get the information that they need to fulfill their visions. It creates a "need to know" that can motivate them throughout the unit.

But how do we decide on an endpoint like the Jerusalem architecture project? Serendipity as much as insight contributes. When we were told that we needed to teach the Middle East, we were overwhelmed by the enormity of the assignment. But one afternoon, Julie stumbled across a book that looked interesting, Moshie Safdie's *Jerusalem: The Future of the Past* (1989). As she leafed through its pages, she thought: Ah ha, here it is. The book jacket described Safdie as an architect who had designed many buildings for Jerusalem after coming to Israel's attention with his work in Montreal Expo '67. A quote from the introduction seemed the perfect challenge for students:

> One cannot build with indifference in Jerusalem. It requires either an act of arrogance—building boldly as Solomon and Herod did— or of aggression—demolishing the old fabric and building anew as the Romans and Umayyads did; or it demands humility—absorbing the past, reflecting upon it, respecting it, as one considers the present and the future. (Safdie 1989, xii)

Inspired, she bought the book and brought the idea to Lynn. Serendipity. At the same time, Lynn had become friends with some architecture students and visual artists and had begun asking questions and looking at pictures and buildings in a more focused, but still casual, way. What she had thought of as only a personal interest—looking at design and form—became a possible entry point for teaching.

With the book as our spark, we soon found ourselves deep in conversation about field trips to develop students' architectural sense and the kinds of information students would need to design and build a scale model structure for Jerusalem. We were engaged and thought our students would be as well—what middle school child doesn't like to build? The project would also demand knowledge and rigorous understanding of the Middle East. An architecture project would simultaneously engage students by allowing them to design any building they wanted, and satisfy our content standards by requiring students to defend their buildings with sound knowledge. And thus our project was born: Design a public use facility for Jerusalem that builds community across diverse populations and is true to Jerusalem's past, present, and future.

Building a Unit Framework

To complete the unit, we knew our students would need background knowledge in several thematic areas: geography, belief systems, current events, literature, and, our vehicle for pulling it all together, architecture. Students would engage in map studies, read and interpret primary source texts, write response journals on a class novel, *Damascus Nights*, by Rafik Schami (1993), conduct Internet research on countries in the region, and maintain an ongoing examination of newspaper coverage of the Palestinian/Israeli conflict. We also identified proficiencies in architecture that would give our students—and ourselves—enough background information in architectural theory and skills to design their buildings in a competent manner: learning how to look at buildings; possessing a shared language for talking about architecture; determining what is important in building design; solving a design problem; producing scale drawings and models; working with precision. Add these skills to how much content we wanted our students to acquire (and then add the number of skills we discovered as we went along) and what we laid out seems like an enormously ambitious project. It was.

We relied on particular resources—in addition to the overarching architectural theme—to tie our complex topic together. For example, from several weeks into the unit up through the final days of the project, we asked our students to be responsible for finding and writing about one newspaper article on the Middle East each week. They used these articles for weekly class discussions in which we built a knowledge of people/individuals, places, and events that played key roles in the region. Our job was to provide our students with the supplemental materials they needed to make sense of the Palestinian/Israeli conflict that unfolded in the newspapers. This meant information on geography, history, politics—international and regional—and journalism, as well as inquiry into the social implications of stereotypes, prejudice, and tolerance.

FIGURE 1–1. Middle East unit plan.

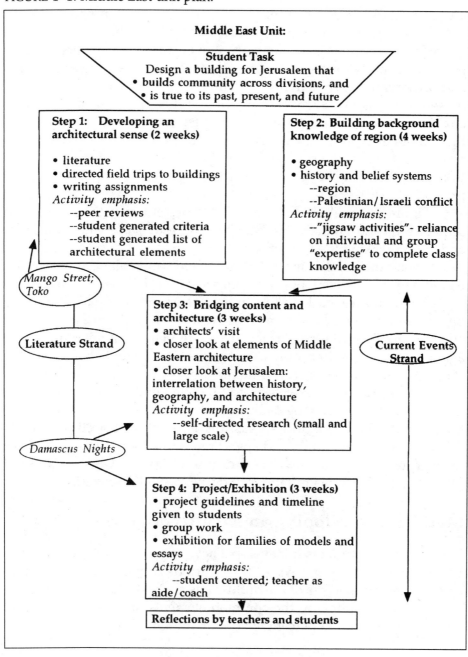

Our reading of *Damascus Nights* illustrates how we also used literature to supplement and complement the current events focus. Rafik Schami is an award-winning Syrian novelist who now lives in Germany. His novel is a magically woven tale that explores Syrian politics in the Nasser era and the tensions between modernization and preservation of a rich, historic culture through a vehicle of one of those traditions, Arab storytelling. In our current political and social environments, most students (and adults!) have greater exposure to the human element of Jewish culture than to Arab culture. We wanted our students to see the beauty and complexity of the Arab world to counter the image of the turbaned terrorist often appearing in our press.

In Figure 1–1 we present a graphic representation that shows the sequence of and connections between the four steps into which we ended up breaking the project.

The diagram makes our work look ordered and balanced; it pictures us moving step-by-step. But our metaphor for ourselves was the circus juggler who dashes back and forth between a series of plates spinning on top of thin canes. Just as one disc begins to wobble and threatens to crash to the floor, the performer arrives to get the momentum going again in the nick of time, only to notice the plate at the other end of the stage teetering precariously. While the unit plan may look as precise as any map, in reality, once we started, we often ended a week saying to each other, "You know, they really need to have more information about the Second World War to address this issue more objectively" or "I think I need to slow down and spend more time with the kids on how to interpret a religious text." Our decision making was constant and often dictated by time limitations and unexpected discoveries.

Step One: Developing an Architectural Sense

We wanted our students to develop a new way of looking at buildings. We wanted them to appreciate how various elements of architecture contribute to the success of the building as a whole. But beginning with an abstract discussion on the common elements of architecture would have alienated a good percentage of our students. We decided to work from what the students already knew. We would identify those elements organically through a series of activities that drew on the knowledge of architecture that is inside of everyone.

To prime the pump, students read descriptions of buildings in two works of fiction. One was a passage from *The House on Mango Street* by Sandra Cisneros, which compared the narrator's current abode to her dream house; the other was from *Potiki* by Patricia Grace, which describes a ceremonial structure built to be accessible to the handicapped narrator. Students thoughtfully identified the feelings that the narrators had toward their buildings—shame in the Cisneros passage, love in the Grace one. Students were struck by the power of the word *there* in the Cisneros passage:

> Once when we were on Loomis, a nun from my school passed by and saw me playing out front. The laundromat downstairs had been boarded up because it had been robbed two days before and the owner had painted on the wood YES WE'RE OPEN so as not to lose business.
>
> Where do you live? she asked.
>
> There, I said pointing up to the third floor.
>
> You live *there*?
>
> *There.* I had to look to where she pointed—the third floor, the paint peeling, wooden bars Papa had nailed on the windows so we wouldn't fall out. You live *there*? The way she said it made me feel like nothing. *There.* I lived *there.* I nodded. (Cisneros 1984, 4)

In contrast, students pointed out the loving detail with which Grace's narrator describes the figures carved in the entranceway to the ceremonial structure:

> My brother James carved the doorway, and in his carvings told the special story of the joining. It is the story of how our people had become as one with the people of Te Ope.
>
> To do this my brother had looked back in the genealogies until he found a common ancestress from whom both people could show descent. He carved the head and shoulders of this ancestress at the centre of the door lintel, showing her to face both

out and in. The two thick, strong arms of the woman stretched out to embrace the two poles that made the door frames on either side. Down these two poles the people were interspersed, the people of our iwi and the people of Te Ope, but linked at the top of the columns by the woman. It was her children that she clasped at either side of her. And these children were working, laughing, crying, singing people, some larger than life. They were young and old, and were joined by their fingers or toes, hands, feet, arms, legs, foreheads or tongues until all had become part of one another. They faced to the hills on the outside, and on the other side they looked in. (Grace 1986, 153)

Students also noted the feelings provoked by particular features of the buildings, such as "windows so small you'd think they were holding their breath" (Cisneros, 4) and "It is a beautiful door that opens without a noise" (Grace, 153). Clearly, there was more to windows and doors than just openings for people and light. By looking so closely at the words and descriptive phrases, students began to realize the influence of society and culture on people's responses to their places.

After reading and discussing these excerpts, we gave our students the following assignment:

Now that you have read and thought about two authors' descriptions of their places, it's your turn. Spend the rest of the period writing about a building or place that you can see clearly in your mind, somewhere that has significance for you. The only rule is that your writing must be *evocative*, that is, it calls forth a strong image, sense, and/or feeling of the place that you describe. So before you write, take a minute to gather your thoughts about this place. Just brainstorm. Once you've gotten a list that you feel is complete, write your description. Use the list as a starting point from which to paint a vibrant picture of your place.

They went home and wrote.

The next day, students read aloud their descriptions of their places and identified all the elements that had provoked a response in them. We combined and refined these lists until we came up with the following list of what we called "architectural elements":

color	lighting
shapes	materials
furniture	windows
decorations	ventilation
entrances and exits	function
layout/flow pattern	words/signage
use of art	sounds/acoustics
landscape	who designed it
designs and symbols	who uses it
who built it	

use of empty space/in-between places
dimensions—height, width, length, depth
relation to other buildings/site

This list stayed up on butcher paper throughout the unit. When we asked professionals, "What did we miss?" they didn't add a single element. We were on our way to becoming architects. Students had a powerful vocabulary that they understood because it was rooted in their personal experiences.

To see how these elements combine in different buildings, we took a series of directed field trips. Since we live in Cambridge, Massachusetts, we had many striking buildings within walking distance. Following each trip, students worked to capture their response to the building in words. Our first trip was a tour of our school and an apartment complex across the street designed by José Luis Sert, a modernist connected with the Gropius movement. We also looked at Memorial Hall at Harvard University, built in the 1870s as a memorial to Harvard students who died in the Civil War. The cavernous transept, marble floors, Latin inscriptions, stained glass, and vaulted ceilings provided a striking contrast to the modern Carpenter Center by Le Corbusier that we walked past on our way. Finally, we went on a walking tour of the neighborhood, looking particularly at shapes, symbols, and form versus function.

Each of these tours was a chance for a lesson in "noticing." We would stop in front of a building and just look. Students would share what they were struck by—lots of windows, a mustard color, peeling paint, a repetition of vertical lines—with the understanding that "I don't know" and "It was boring" weren't acceptable responses. These sharing sessions served as a safety net for students less confident in their observational powers. We would discuss the effect of these features on us; students would take notes as we looked and talked. When possible, we went in, noticing where and how we entered and what our eyes were drawn to as we entered. We also paid attention to where our eyes wandered once inside and tried to identify why they did so. By the end of the three trips, students' conversations and opinions flowed easily. The students were beginning to put the language to use, forming ideas about what they were seeing and adding to our list of architectural elements as we discovered new aspects to architecture and design.

By the end of the week, students had written four pieces about responses to architecture. We wanted our students to revise their pieces to refine both their writing skills and push their thinking about architecture. We also kept in mind the criteria implied by one of our original planning questions: How would we engage our students by opening up the options for expression as opposed to limiting them? And besides, we weren't insane—we couldn't evaluate four pieces of writing from each student. So we asked them to select the piece that they were most interested in and revise that. We developed a set of criteria and a peer review format that could be used for all pieces (see Figure 1–2).

At the end of the several days of writing, critiquing, and revising, we saw that the noticing had worked. Alex Valdez' piece is typical of their products. He clearly revised, eliminating unnecessary details and refining his word choice; his writing also illustrates a solid appreciation of architectural features in the details he chooses to focus on. In his first draft he wrote:

> As I left the train station at Harvard Square on a Monday morning everything was quiet. It's not like at 3:00 pm when everything is loud and rambunctious traffic is everywhere. Alot of people are smoking but now it's like a ghost town. Cars are less. You can hear your shows hitting the ground. It's so quiet I wonder how things are in central sq. I could have gone that way but I'm late for school and Harvard's my first stop on the redline. As I get to Putnam Ave., I see one other late student. I feel a little bit

FIGURE 1–2. Criteria for place writing.

Place Writing--Criteria

Capable: Writing displays evidence of the following characteristics
- clearly identifiable place;
- addresses five (5) of the architectural elements;
- includes some interpretation of elements;
- organized so that reader can follow ideas;
- solid mechanics which do not distract from the reading.

Very Proficient: Writing meets criteria for *capable* **and:**
- details chosen, developed and organized to contribute to an overall feeling or experience;
- incorporates at least two suggestions from the peer review;
- well proofed for mechanics (typos, spelling, grammar, punctuation, etc.).

Going Beyond: Writing meets criteria for *very proficient* **and:**
- comes across as a tightly written whole, in which details, word choices, organization and grammar all contribute to cohesion of piece;
- shows evidence of an ability to revise work on one's own;
- shows analysis and/or appreciation of architectural decisions.

Overall Impression: What do you like most about this piece of writing?

What should the author work on most?

---

of a relief because I'm not the only person 1 hour late for school. That's what I get for going to bed at 2 AM and watching t.v. As I keep on walking down Putnam Ave I can see the white fence in front of the school. As I take a turn I can imagine a private path to get in the school. I pull open the green doors and woosh! A gust of hot air hits me and I see light trying to light up the hall.

Here is his revision:

As I left the train station at Harvard Square on a Monday morning, everything was quiet. It's not like at 3:00 pm when everything is loud and ranbunctious. Traffic is everywhere. A lot of people are smoking but now it's like a ghost town. You can't hear a thing. It's so quiet you can hear your shoes hitting the ground as you walk. I wonder how things are in Central Square. I could have gone that way but I'm late for school and Harvard's my first stop off the Red Line. As I get to Putnam Ave., I see one other late student. I feel a little bit of relief because I'm not the only person one hour late for school. That's what I get for going to bed at 2:00 am and watching T.V.

As I keep walking down Putnam Ave. I can see the white fence in front of the school. As I take the turn I can imagine a private path to get in the school. I pull open the green doors and voosh!—a gust of hot air hits me. I see dim lights trying to light up the hall. My body slowly adapts to the frigid air from the ten degree weather. As I walk in I can adjust right away because the hall is so alive. I look to my right as I see the silhouettes from the mural of the Civil Rights Movement. A light hits me in the face which causes me to look up and see the slanted ceiling and skylights. When I view the ceiling I imagine myself in a triangle. Focusing down the hallway, I imagine that big hall as being the hub of a wheel and all the rooms are the spokes. I hear hello's and how are you's everywhere which gives me a good feeling from the people. It's as if I knew each and every one of them. After walking down the hall, I see that the use of the hall is not just for walking but for hanging up art work.

At the end of the day I feel I've left a colorful, lively and very good planet. Outside was outer space—empty, dead, and boring.

The variety of the work satisfied us that students were not stifled. Step One had gone well.

Step Two: Building Background Knowledge

It was time to focus on building background knowledge of the region. We began by asking students "What would you need to know in order to meet the design challenge we've given you?" Their answers committed them to exploring geography, history, belief systems, and current events of the Middle East—the same thematic areas that we had come up with ourselves in our original planning session. This was a significant step in our quest for engagement. Students were already investing in developing what we call *knowing in general* and *knowing for a purpose* (e.g., to design their buildings).

There were more signs of engagement during our first focus of study: geography, the physical world around any building. Using blank maps and a list of countries, cities, landforms, and bodies of water, students mapped out the Middle East. Then we assigned each student a country. We made a transparency of the blank map and projected it on the board. Each student traced an enlarged version of their country onto oaktag, creating one piece in a big class puzzle of the Middle East. Students searched the library and the Internet for information about their country: climate, important cities, language, type of government, and so forth. While they worked on finding the required information, they colored in the deserts on their puzzle pieces, located cities, and made replicas of flags. Then we played games, constructing the Middle East over and over again on the floor of our rooms. We knew that the image of the Middle East as a puzzle was working when, as the "puzzle pieces" were near completion, a student doing Syria began wandering around the room looking for connecting pieces. "Who has Saudi Arabia? What about Israel?" Soon, she had two thirds of the class clustered around her, other students intently fitting the countries together and calling for other countries to be brought by. As they stepped back to admire their work, a near complete map of the Middle East resplendent in the colors and designs that only seventh and eighth graders can come up with, the original instigator observed, "Saudi Arabia really ties it all together, doesn't it?"

As students learned the "geography," they also practiced their research skills using a variety of sources, became class resources for information on their countries, and had fun. We tied this process to our architecture objectives by having them look on the Internet for pictures of buildings in their individual countries and formulate ideas about how location, climate, and population might have affected the structures they found. We wrapped up our geography study with a test and moved into our next thematic content area: belief systems.

During the previous semester we had taught China and loved the experience we had interpreting primary texts with our students. We had read excerpts from the *Tao Te Ching*, the Confucian *Analects*, and the Buddhist *Pali Canon*, and students had "translated" the central ideas within them. We wanted our students to engage with language that was unfamiliar to them and to struggle with finding a strategy for figuring out what it meant. Because we feel it is important to allow students to practice proficiencies over time, and because we like the students to develop a familiarity with our structures, we repeated this process in our Middle East unit. The students began by reading from a secondary source about Judaism and Islam, learning about themes present in each religion, those that are shared and those that are different. Then we went to the Torah and the Koran, decoding the language (often word by word), and looking for echoes of the themes they had identified from their previous reading. To practice these interpretive skills further, each group (we do much of our work in small groups of four or five students) received one or two passages to explore together. They had to figure out the meaning and then to write any portions of their selection that related to the identified themes on sheets of chart paper taped up around the room. We had labeled the paper in advance with these themes. The students had to make connections, and then we asked them to defend them. The rest of the class gave their opinions and interpretations as each group introduced and explained their excerpt.

We connected our study of belief systems to our architecture study by having students look for cultural and religious symbolism in buildings, not only in pictures of the Middle East, but in Cambridge. Do we see any cultural or religious themes translated into architectural elements? This opened the door for us to assign a writing piece on the family or individual symbols that held significance for each student. We found that, eventually, we didn't have to force personal or content connections: the students were doing it for us.

When a somewhat reluctant student came in with a page of editorial cartoons about the Middle East peace process, proud that he understood them, or when another student brought in books about Jerusalem, or when other students approached us and said, "Did you see the news last night? Netanyahu was on!" we knew we had succeeded in getting students to invest in the learning process. Creating a knowledge base became easier and easier as the students developed more and varied ways of linking together the information they were encountering, another benefit to interdisciplinary curriculum planning. Again, we were learning along with our students, seeing our environment in a more complex way.

Step Three: Bridging Architecture and Content

We now focused our content and activities on bridging the different kinds of knowledge we were building with the region and its architecture. The students were starting to buzz about their own buildings. Early in the unit, we had leaked information about the final stage of this unit, where we would build a scale model of a building. As the unit progressed, we kept referring to this project, and students began creating their own mental files of preferences and design ideas. We were also excited, sharing our students' insights with each other in amazement and appreciation. But now we had to start thinking about teaching drafting, something neither of us knew anything about.

Again we had to find experienced people to help us. Fortunately, we had parents who worked as architects who we knew would help us out. They graciously taught a lesson on design for the students, beginning with a detailed description of what architects really do. As they talked, they emphasized meeting deadlines. Much to our delight, they ended with a real design task, an outdoor stage in a public park that came with a fixed set of criteria: dimensions, capacity, landscaping, traffic flow. The students grouped up and began to discuss and draw, using architectural tracing paper. Unfortunately, we ran out of time for the full group critique. But it was clear that our students loved to problem solve using the concrete visual medium of architecture. They were hooked and so were we.

Our next challenge was to merge our exploration of architecture with our study of the region. Since neither of us knew much about architecture of the Middle East, we again went to search out help. The Center for Middle Eastern Studies at Harvard has a teaching resource center run by a wonderfully knowledgeable staff person, Carol Shedd. Carol lent us books from the Center's rich collection on Islamic architecture, along with a few videotapes about the great mosques of Sinan, architect to the Ottoman ruler Suleiman. We used these resources in class to take a closer look at the elements of Middle Eastern architecture, reading about mosques and exploring the architectural and cultural features of Sinan's works.

We also intensified our focus on Jerusalem and the interrelation of history, geography, and architecture in that city. For this, the computer was an invaluable resource. Our students looked for pictures of buildings in Middle Eastern countries on the Internet. They were eager to share what they found: ancient bridges, contemporary appliance stores, schools and university buildings, modern art museums, houses. We also took a virtual tour of the Old City of Jerusalem that let students "visit" archaeological and contemporary building sites in the city, and read about the historic periods in which they were built. Students brought in books from home on architecture and Jerusalem. Our Muslim students shared their knowledge of mosques and Islamic symbolism, our Jewish students talked about synagogues, and one student's mother, a minister, let her son bring in her snapshots of her trip to Jerusalem.

We started to look at and read about traditional elements in Islamic architecture: the domes of Sinan, stonework, materials, layout. But we were running out of time and we weren't sure about how to prioritize. Our students needed to start planning for their buildings. We ended up just leaving the vast range of resources that Carol had lent us in the rooms for students to investigate. It was one of those lucky mistakes: students love to look, and they used these books often throughout the remainder of the unit.

Step Four: Project/Exhibition

It was time to focus our energies on the project, now with specific guidelines and time lines. Figure 1–3 is the assignment sheet we handed our students, Figure 1–4 is the time line.

FIGURE 1–3. Architecture Assignment project sheet.

Architecture Project: Building Community

"One cannot build with indifference in Jerusalem. It requires either an act of arrogance—building boldly as Solomon and Herod did; or of aggression—demolishing the old fabric and building anew as the Romans and the Umayyads did; or it demands humility—absorbing the past, reflecting upon it, respecting it, as one considers the present and future."
Moshe Safdie, *Jerusalem: The Future of the Past*.
(Houghton Mifflin, 1989).

Task
Design a building for Jerusalem that is true to its past, present, and future and that builds community across divisions. Your building will need to fit into one of three site options:
1. Urban plot, commercially zoned, surrounded by modern buildings;
2. Residentially zoned plot, surrounded by older buildings and homes, some dating back to very early in Jerusalem's history;
3. An underdeveloped hilltop site on the edges of the city proper.

You may work individually or in groups of no more than three. The project will involve several stages, described below; each stage will have specific criteria built from its description that we will discuss in more detail as we go. You are responsible for completing all of the stages. So reflect on what you've learned about the Middle East and architecture so far, keep your eyes and ears open for new and helpful information and ideas, and start creating!

Stage One: Proposal
Make a formal proposal for your building. Your proposal must include the following:
1. Proposed building (what it will be, how it will be used, who will use it) and building site (including justification for the site);
2. Explanation of how your structure will build community across divisions;
3. Explanation of how your building connects to Jerusalem's past, present, and future.
Format: Written and oral presentation

FIGURE 1–3 (CONT.). Architecture Assignment project sheet.

Stage Two: Sketch to Scale

Prepare a to-scale sketch of your building, in color. You must sketch your building from at least two perspectives. On the sketch you need to identify the following:

1. Exits and entrances;
2. Landscape features.

In addition, you need to have a written justification of the following elements;

1. Building materials: what are you using and why are those good choices?
2. Four (4) design decisions; you must justify these in terms of the project's two essential questions: How do your design decisions help the building be true to Jerusalem's past, present, and future, and How do they contribute to the building of community across divisions?

Stage Three: Final Products

Model: You will build a to-scale model of your building. We will discuss as a class specific criteria for the model.

Conceptual Presentation of Building: This is an essay (at least three pages) in which you formally present how your building satisfies the project's two essential questions and how you justify your site decision. One essay per model; the essay needs to go through a minimum of one draft and peer review before the final draft.

Individual Reflection: A written reflection (minimum 1 1/2 pages) in which you reflect on the group process and your contribution to it.

Presentation: You will present your model and other products formally to the school community. Each member of the group must participate in oral explanations to your audience.

FIGURE 1–4. Architecture Project checklist.

Name(s) _____
Section _____

Architecture Project: Building Community
Checklist and Project Due Dates

	Individual Contributions		
	Student	Student	Student
	_____	_____	_____

Stage One
Group Proposal   Due 5/2
_____ Written Proposal | | _____ | _____ | _____ |
_____ Presentation for approval | | _____ | _____ | _____ |

Stage Two
_____ Individual Sketches Due 5/5   _____   _____   _____

_____ Group Sketch   Due 5/9   _____   _____   _____
Rough Draft and Peer Review
Includes written piece

_____ Final Sketch   Due 5/16   _____   _____   _____
Includes written piece

Stage Three
_____ Peer Review of Model As Is   _____   _____   _____
Due 5/23
_____ Peer Review of Writing Draft _____   _____   _____
Due 5/27
Final Work Days   6/2 and 6/3

Final Due Date - 6/4
____ **Presentation**   _____   _____   _____
____ **Model Finished**   _____   _____   _____
____ **Essay Finished**   _____   _____   _____
____ **Individual Reflection** _____   _____   _____

For Individual Participation:
+ = provided leadership in this area
√ = contributed ideas and opinions, helped with the work
− = did not contribute much to the process in this area
0 = interfered with the completion of this step

We reminded students of the charge: designing a public use building for Jerusalem that takes into consideration the architectural traditions of the region, both secular and sacred; historical information; geographic concerns (location and climate); and a sensitivity for the current conflict.

Students worked in self-selected groups for the concrete process of creating. They first wrote proposals, which needed to be approved by their classmates. This allowed us to reopen our ongoing discussions about criteria. (A central part of our Humanities course was engaging with students in discussions about quality work before they completed it.) We posed the question "What will make a good proposal?" and students came up with three basic criteria: the proposal addresses the requirements; it is convincing (i.e., presented confidently, seems to be thought through); and it is realistic enough that the structure could really be built.

The initial requirements had come from us; however, students had to present their proposals to the class, not to us. The class decided whether or not the proposal met the criteria to an adequate standard. Not every proposal passed the first group presentation. One student wanted to build a prison. The class was incredulous. How does a prison build community across divisions, one of the basic components to the assignment? However, he was able to prove that his idea met all but that one requirement, and he had really done his homework. He went back to the drawing board and returned the next day with a prison that housed a community policing program and a mediation center. The class approved his proposal. They didn't all agree that it met the spirit of the assignment, but they felt that it did meet the criteria they had helped design.

From here students went through a series of design stages before actually building their models. They did rough sketches to start the visualization process. Bernardo's sketch is remarkable both in his use of perspective and for how it captures the design process in motion (Figure 1–5).

Students then completed more formal scale drawings. Heather's drawing in Figure 1–6 shows an extraordinary attention to details in her community center.

Lauren, Kate, Cinta, and Maria took pains to follow architectural conventions in their scale drawing, going so far as to indicate the thickness of walls and materials used (Figure 1–7).

FIGURE 1–5. Bernardo's sketch.

FIGURE 1–6. Heather's community center drawing.

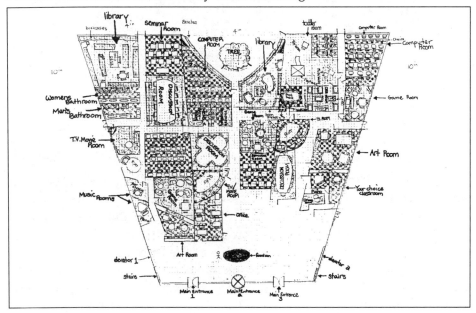

FIGURE 1–7. Detailed drawing by Lauren, Kate, Cinta, and Maria.

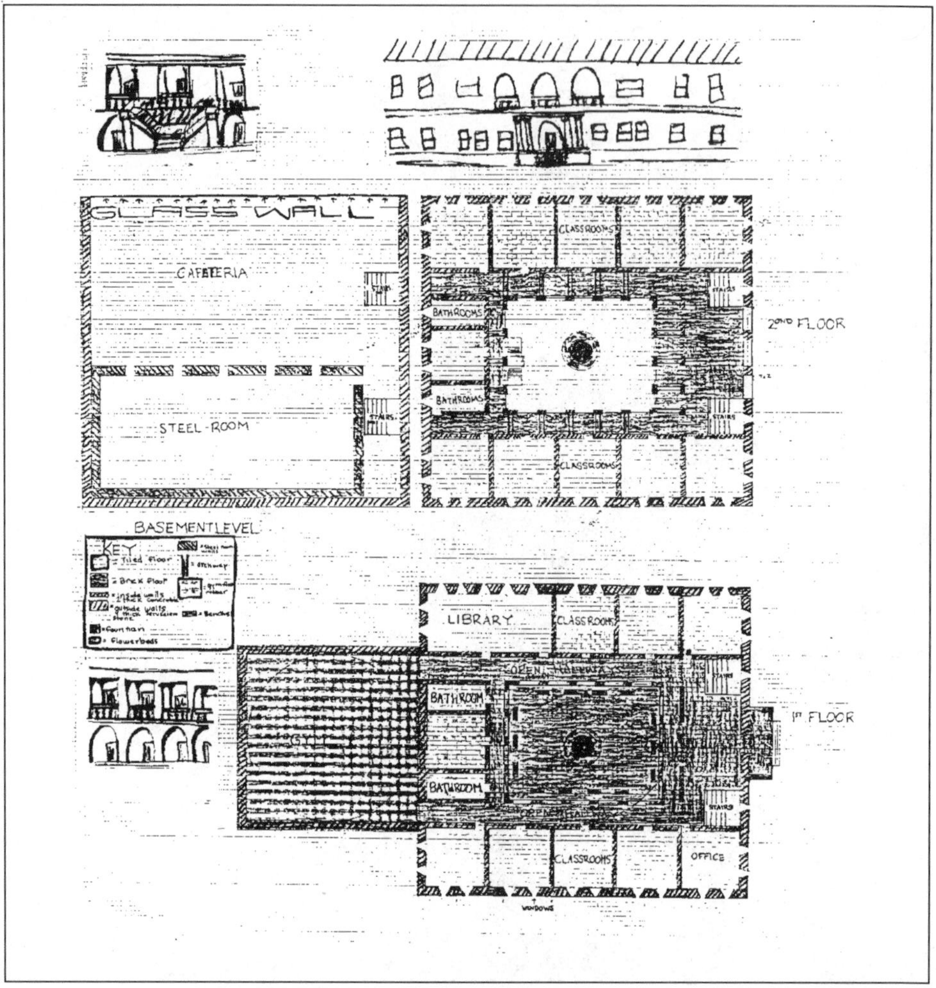

The use of criteria was immensely important to the project. The more we talked about criteria in our classes and defended our reasons for holding certain standards, the more competent the kids became at contributing to the criteria-building process. The criteria lists we used to evaluate the students on the final stages of their projects came from full class discussions about what would make these quality products. In essence, they set the standards for themselves. And the expectations were rigorous and comprehensive (see Figures 1–8 and 1–9).

FIGURE 1–8. Sketch and writing criteria.

Stage Two: Sketch to Scale

To receive a "capable," a sketch must
- be drawn from two perspectives/views
- use scale accurately
- have entrances and exits clearly marked
- clearly show any landscape elements
- be in color
- be neat and clearly labeled
- include orientation; North arrow.

To receive a "very proficient," a sketch must meet all of the criteria for a capable *and*
- show attention to details; designs, shows dimension in some way, placement of furniture, etc.
- have a key to help reader interpret the sketch
- is proofed for errors.

To receive a "going beyond," a sketch must meet all of the criteria for a "very proficient" *and*
- include views or details that highlight important elements: e.g., how two walls meet in an interesting way or a close up view of a mosaic edging a window
- be presented creatively and very neatly.

To receive a "capable," a writing piece
- discusses building materials; what and why
- addresses four design elements in terms of "building community across divisions" and Jerusalem's past, present, and future
- is evidence of organized writing and solid form; introduction, body, conclusion
- uses solid mechanics that do not distract.

continued

FIGURE 1–8 (CONT.). Sketch and writing criteria.

To receive a "very proficient," a writing piece must meet all of the criteria for a "capable" *and*
- is engaging writing; introduction draws the reader in, the body supports with specific examples and details, conclusion leaves reader with an idea to consider
- well-proofread, no typos.

To receive a "going beyond," a writing piece must meet all of the criteria for a "very proficient" *and*
- uses comparisons and connections that show deeper understanding of the regions of our theme questions from climate to social structure to architecture
- shows control of language, strong word choices, and structure that create a cohesive whole
- gives credit to sources.

Deciding on criteria with our students takes time, but it is a process that we value enormously. It lets the students know up front what is expected of them. The teacher is no longer imbued with the mysterious power of giving that final grade. We rarely agonize over a student's evaluation now. We look at our criteria and trust in their integrity. And so do the students. The students know why they receive the grade they do: it's right there in front of them. They also are more invested in meeting the standards. After all, they set them. And finally, we believe in this process as an academic skill. We want our students to develop the ability to set standards, make evaluations, distinguish between a capable piece of work and one that is very proficient, and to think about all of the aspects of quality. We don't need them to agree universally on definitions of quality, but we do want them to consider the question and realize that they are able to have an informed discussion of standards. Our hope is that this process moves inward, so that students begin to set standards for themselves and that they endeavor to meet them.

But even as our students worked, we were having some doubts about the task we had given them. One of the fortunate and uncontrol-

FIGURE 1–9. Model and essay criteria.

Stage Three: Model and Essay

To receive a "capable," a model must
- meet the deadline
- use scale accurately and reasonably (1"=10')
- provide a basic sense of the structure and form of the building
- include the highlighted four design choices
- have entrances and exits clearly marked
- clearly show any landscape elements
- be in color
- clearly show building material choices
- show stable construction overall
- include orientation; North arrow
- be neat and clearly labeled; presentable
- include a key for elements that aren't clear from looking.

To receive a "very proficient," a model must meet all of the criteria for a "capable" *and*
- use scale *very* accurately
- show dimension in some way
- show attention to environment or site in some way
- is very neat and accurate, stable and clean lines
- reveal interior in some way; cutaways, removable roof, missing wall
- use accurate color that reveals building materials.

To receive a "going beyond," a model must meet all of the criteria for a "very proficient" *and*
- have a detailed interior
- come with supplemental materials; detail sketches, advertising, other additional information, additional models of details, pictures of sources of ideas
- show engineering elements/construction
- show lighting.

FIGURE 1–9 (CONT.). Model and essay criteria.

To receive a "capable," an essay must
- be at least five pages long
- discuss building materials in depth; what and why
- make connections to Jerusalem's past, present, and future
- discuss at least four specific design choices; what and why
- explore how the building "builds community across divisions," with specific attention to individual design choices
- justify the site
- is written in standard essay form; an introduction, body, conclusion, and transitions
- must show solid mechanics that do not distract; spelling, punctuation, and grammar (Have someone else proofread for you!)

To receive a "very proficient," an essay must meet all of the criteria for a "capable" and
- answer the overall question, "Why do you want to build this particular building?"
- go into depth about the use of the building
- include at least two references to the sources for ideas
- the writing is engaging and well organized; the introduction has a solid lead and shows the thesis or angle, each paragraph in the body has only one idea which is supported with examples and details, the conclusion ties the piece together and leaves reader with an idea to consider
- show a thoughtful attempt at using transitions
- well-proofread, no typos.

To receive a "going beyond," an essay must meet all of the criteria for a "very proficient" and
- use comparisons and connections that show deeper understanding of the region or our theme questions: from the Middle East to American politics to community service to China
- show evidence of beautifully used language; strong word choices that are specific and precise, simile/metaphor, personification, strong verbs that are specific, intentional use of structure to set a tone
- give credit to at least five sources for ideas
- hang together in a cohesive whole with a connecting thread throughout.

lable aspects of teaching, especially teaching a topic for the first time, is that you end up learning and caring about the content in a way you hadn't before you started. Our current events newspaper study had an unexpected effect on our excitement about our project. We were looking closely, along with our students, at the political realities and human struggles of the peoples involved in conflict in Jerusalem. As a result, we became concerned about our assignment to design a building project for Jerusalem. The implications became more clear as we followed the news. While we studied architecture in Cambridge in preparation for our buildings, an Israeli housing project in East Jerusalem was quickly becoming an international symbol of conflicting national aspirations. The very premise of breaking ground in Jerusalem came to carry a symbolic weight that we were uncomfortable with as time went on. Sections of Jerusalem are contested ground, and having our students enter into a project of this type began to feel presumptuous. We were too far into our quagmire at this point to pull out, but our concerns remain. Though our students were well informed and sensitive to complex issues, we felt that there was a trivializing aspect to our project, a problem we need to address before we teach the project again.

Reflections on the Final Products

Our students managed, with much bustle and not a few frustrating moments, to complete their models in time for an exhibition for families and community members. The following photos show the range in the students' projects—from a woman's health facility in a wooded park to a domed mall with a working elevator.

It was a proud night. They took turns sitting by their displays and answering questions for viewers about design features and historical references. They also milled around, delighting in the finished products of their peers. Judging from the general festive air of the event, as well as from the glowing compliments for our young architects on feedback sheets put up next to their displays, the evening was a success.

Yet, while the warm feelings of such events are nice, we want more concrete ways of evaluating our teaching. We had taken several months of our students' time; was it worth it? We look to the student work and outside interpretation of that work for answers to that question. The fol-

FIGURE 1–10A. Women's health center.

FIGURE 1–10B. Domed mall.

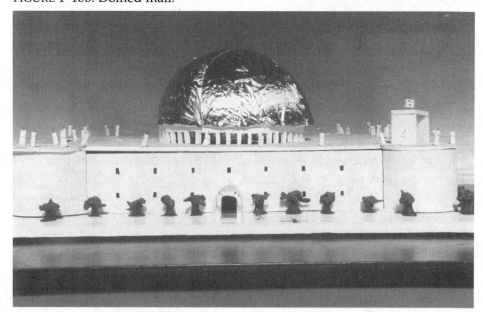

lowing excerpts from three student essays are representative of the knowledge and thinking that student products displayed. (They are only excerpts, since the essays ranged from five to ten pages!)

Jerusalem is a city, but it's not just a city. It is a religious center to Judaism, Islam, and Christianity. In this city Jesus was crucified, it was here that Muhammed ascended into heaven, and both of Judaism's Temples were built inside Jerusalem's walls. For millennia different cultures have lived here and for millennia there has been strife. I can not classify the different parties who are fighting. If I said Jews and Moslems that would not be true, if I said Israelis and Palestinians, that would also not be true, since not all the Jews are fighting the Moslems and vice versa. As you see the different factions aren't divided solely on religious lines (nationalities are divisors too). However, much of their motivation for wanting the land is religious.

   Somehow the land is not big enough for each of the warring parties to live in it together. Yet Anwar el-Sadat (the Egyptian president who made peace with Israel) said "Peace is more important than a piece of land." The first step to peace is understanding, understanding yourself and understanding others. The means to understand yourself are readily available, however the means to understand others are not. And what better way to learn about others than a library? This is what my building is, a library. And since much of the problem at hand is related to religion, all the books in my library will be related to religion. . . .

   . . . My building will be constructed out of steel and glass and faced with Jerusalem stone. Jerusalem stone is a pale yellow limestone found only in Israel. It gives off a golden glow when sunlight hits it. Almost all of the old city is constructed out of this material. The roof of my building is constructed out of red tile. This style of roof was brought to the Middle East from Europe. It was sloped to withstand northern snowstorms, even though snowstorms are not as frequent here as in the north. Both Jews and Moslems adopted this style of building, and soon it became common all over the Middle East. . . .

   . . . I also tried to build community across divisions architecturally, instead of just having it be a purpose of my building. And so I came up with an element that not only relates to all three time periods mentioned previously, but builds community across divisions. This element is the floor of my library. It is a huge mosaic of the old city. As people walk over this hopefully they will be inspired to think that this city houses many different religions and is holy to all of them, and hopefully it will also inspire them to think about peace. . . .

Alex Grabner

The headline of an article on the front page of last February's *Boston Globe* read, "Palestinians killed in clash" (*Boston Globe*, 2/26/97), another headline in last April's Globe read, "Three dead in West Bank strife" (*Globe*, 4/10/97). These headlines are some of many that for the past 80 years have been on the front pages of our newspapers, revealing the violence that has been going on in Israel, in particularly Jerusalem, between the Palestinians and the Jews. Since 1918, Jerusalem has acted as sort of a large battlefield on which the Palestinians and the Jews have fought over the land, each group believing that the land is rightfully theirs. These fights over land have escalated to the point where there is much fear and hate between the Jews and the Palestinians. This escalated fear and hate has lead many people to examine the Palestinian and Israeli conflict, and has lead many people to ask what they can do. In Humanities we decided that we could design buildings for Jerusalem that might in the future improve the status between the Jews and the Palestinians. With the chance to design a building in Jerusalem, we decided to create a three part building, in which there will be a mediation facility, a meditation center, and a bookstore. In addition to the three main parts of the building, we have included four architectural building decisions, and varied materials that will help to achieve the goals of our building. In this project our goals are to create a building that builds community across religious and cultural divisions, and in doing so, build a building that architecturally connects to the past, present, and future. Each of the three parts of our building, each architectural decision and every material we use, will help to achieve our goals and improve the peace process in Jerusalem and the Middle East. . . .

. . . Our second building decision is to have a triangular pyramid on top of our large tower that will be our mediation facility. The pyramid will be modern in style and made of metal. The idea for having the metal pyramid came from the recently built Supreme Court Building in Jerusalem. The architects of Israel's Supreme Court building, Ram Carmi and Ada Carmi-Melemed, decided on building a metal pyramid on top of a glass tower that is positioned above the main entrance to the Supreme Court building. We, like Carmi and Melemed, believe metal is a strong material that will hold up well, and that it ties in with the skyline of Jerusalem. Inside we want people to get the feeling that they are in a high tower surrounded by people trying to make peace. The pyramid will contribute to accentuate the height of the tower. At the top of the tower, where the sides of the triangle come together, there will be a large plaque. This plaque will have on it the names of every person and group that comes together and works out their problems and makes a resolution in one of the mediation rooms in our tower under our pyramid. The shape of the pyramid has symbolic value as well. Just as the sides of a pyramid come together, individuals of diverse communities will come together. Our metal pyramid will draw people from outdoors to our mediation center, where they will come together, and make peace, and earn their spot on the plaque that lies on top of our six-flapped pyramid. . . .

Adam Poswolski

Jerusalem and its people have been through many hardships and struggles over the city's history. Conflict and anger have penetrated the city's walls and have buried themselves deep in the heart of Jerusalem. Our building is designed to tackle this problem head on, and although we couldn't solve it alone, we can make a step towards a lasting peace.

Our building, a library and a community center, is designed with several elements chosen to build community across divisions and also incorporate the past, present, and future in the architecture. . . .

. . . We did some research to find typical designs in religious or cultural buildings from certain groups of people and throughout history. We found that domes were very common not only in many Christian churches from an early period (the sixth century Santa Sophia in Istanbul, for example), but also in Islamic mosques, having become especially predominant in Ottoman architecture, with the introduction of the dome-on-square style. Domes also became common in a style of one large dome and surrounding smaller domes, similar to, for example, Caliph Suleiman (an Ottoman ruler from 1520 to 1566) and his court. This information determined our connection to Islamic and Christian architecture, but we wanted to connect to Jewish style as well.

Because of the Diaspora, or scattering of the Jews over history, they have not established a distinctive architectural style, and therefore it was hard to connect our building architecturally to Judaism. However, in a sketch of a Jewish temple, we found an arched entryway we had not seen many times before and decided to incorporate it into our building. Thus we had found elements for the major religions in Jerusalem.

Much of the architecture of the past is connected to religion, and by far the majority of people living in Jerusalem today are strongly involved in their religions. Because of this, we hoped that when entering, Jews, Muslims, and Christians would feel at home as well as people of other faiths. We were careful not to include too many elements from one religion or group, as that might cause separation which is the exact opposite of what we are aiming for. These elements connect to the past, but we also connected our building to the future. . . .

Lucy Lindsey and Lucilla Haskovec

We like to ask for outside evaluations of the learning that is evidenced in student work because we are often so intimately involved in the process that we lose track of what is truly in the work and what is merely in our memory of encounters and conversations with students along the way. The visitors to our classroom on the final days of our preparation had a chance to see the student products at a later date. When we asked them what they saw of value, they came up with the following list:

- students are engaged;
- students work together to solve problems;
- students integrate knowledge from a wide range of sources;
- students are showing individual ideas of how to meet the project's challenge;
- their sketches are very detailed and thoughtful;
- their models are very professional-looking and creative;
- there is a lot of history in the essays;
- students seem to respect the cultures they are talking about;
- students had to do a lot of research to produce their projects;
- students seem very proud of their work.

One of our primary goals is to engage students in a depth of study significant enough to entitle them to speak about someone else's culture. Overall, we were pleased with what we saw in our students' products and gratified that others seemed to see the exact qualities that we valued in those products as well. Our original planning questions helped us get these results: our students had learned what we felt was significant; they were engaged enough to seek out information to enrich their products; the resources that we used were varied and valid as well as helpful in allowing students to go deeper in their individual explorations.

This depth of learning is contagious. It kept us thinking about our own questions about choosing Jerusalem and its conflicts as the center of our teaching on the Middle East. We are still left wondering: Have we inadvertently encouraged our students to seek a pat solution to a complex issue, e.g., designing a building to resolve the Palestinian/Israeli conflict? We need to address this question the next time we teach our unit. We loved the energy and excitement with which students tackled their research and designs, and we don't want to lose those qualities. But we need to do the work necessary to incorporate more of the perspectives of people who are intimately involved in the crisis. We are particularly concerned about the depth of our presentation of Arab perspectives, given the current tenor of media coverage of the Middle East. We hope to develop e-mail connections with Arab children, or have Palestinian/Israeli dialogue groups talk to our students. Borders do exist between people. It's not our job to ignore the distinctions, but to help our students understand them as fully as possible. Our hope is that the more resources and disciplines we can weave together in our studies, the closer we can come to realizing that full understanding.

References

Cisneros, Sandra. 1984. *The House on Mango Street*. New York: Vintage Books.

Grace, Patricia. 1986. *Potiki*. Auckland, New Zealand: Penguin Books.

Safdie, Moshie. 1989. *Jerusalem: The Future of the Past*. Boston: Houghton Mifflin.

Schami, Rafik. 1993. *Damascus Nights*. New York: Farrar, Straus & Giroux. Originally published in German under the title, *Erzaler der Nacht*, in 1989 by Beltz Verlag, Weinham and Basel.

Response from a Colleague:
Building Up a Sense of Place

Larry Bauer

Every field of human endeavor has a core understanding at its heart. Those understandings define the essence, the genius, and the responsibilities of that field. At the very heart of architecture, there is a "sense of place." It is this sense that allows us to recognize, create, preserve, honor, or renew the spaces that make up the built environment we share.

In some ways we are most alert to our sense of place when it has been violated. A good example is the high-rise public housing that was built in cities across the United States in the 1950s and 1960s. People in Chicago actually cheered when, at last, some of those projects were blown up.

We also become aware of this sense of place when it is endangered or challenged. For instance, whenever an architect like me enters a community commissioned to build a large public building like a museum or a library, people want to know whether I can see what their place is about and whether I will respect it. For instance, I was part of a team designing a new museum in Albany. It was to connect and fill the space between two nineteenth-century brick buildings of the kind that give the historic district of Albany its character as a place. Residents, along with the historical commission, were anxious that the new structure not destroy that character. As architects, that gave us our design challenge: build a contemporary museum that belongs in old-time Albany. As a solution, we designed a structure almost entirely of glass, connecting the two brick buildings, without hiding any of their important features.

In designing a new museum for Charleston, South Carolina, we also had a very particular place to respect—an old Southern city. The design solution continued the Charleston tradition by separating the new building into several distinct components, enclosing and forming the walls of a garden courtyard visible through iron gates, and closing the gaps between building components. The courtyard and other land-scaped areas around the structure were filled with plants from the region and landscaped by people who have been planting Charleston gardens for years. The museum was built of brick closely matching the color and texture of the brick used in nearby historic houses and the height of the building was set to match the wall height of an adjacent historic house. To have a sense of place is to have a form of respect, an ability to understand the history, the materials, the structures, and the symbols of a community.

Even though I am years and years away from middle school, what I immediately liked and respected about Lynn Brown and Julie Craven's work on Jerusalem was how important that sense of place was to the project. The Jerusalem project is a curriculum for developing the sense of place I am talking about. The walks through Cambridge and the readings are just the right sort of beginning. The study of geography, climate, and history provide the sort of tools and knowledge necessary. The model building demands translating understandings into struc-tures. Even the essay, I can see as a way of urging reflection about the kinds of choices the particular building represents.

As an architect, I do have one idea about how students' sense of place could be expanded. There is no client for the students' buildings in the Jerusalem project. There is no equivalent to the historical commission in Albany or the neighbors in Charleston. I think there ought to be—and not just because that is how architects really work. When I talk about devel-oping a sense of place it sounds almost like seeing—a kind of perception that belongs to an individual. But it is much more like a conversation. My sense of place is provoked and sharpened by being asked to enhance, not obscure, the nineteenth-century museum buildings in Albany.

Suppose students had a local group of parents or neighbors with knowledge of the type of building the students had chosen. This "client" group could talk with the students about how the building is used, how it would fit into community life, and how it might reflect its values and its sense of place. The client group might also include an architect to help the students translate client input into built form. Or better yet, suppose the students were in touch with other students and clients in Israel who could critique and make suggestions. Imagine that those Israeli clients included Jews, Arabs, and Christians. That would give students the chance to develop the skills to design in the way that Safdie calls for:

> One can not build with indifference in Jerusalem. It requires either an act of arrogance—building boldly as Solomon and Herod did—or of aggression—demolishing the old fabric and building anew as the Romans and Umayyads did; or it demands humility—absorbing the past, reflecting upon it, respecting it, as one considers the present and the future. (Safdie 1989, xii)

2

Going Up to Harlem

Understanding an American Renaissance

Karen Sorin

My favorite movie has always been *The Miracle Worker.* Annie Sullivan is my role model; she never gave up. She would teach Helen Keller. Annie's pleading question was always, "How do I reach you!?"

The New School of Orlando opened its doors in downtown Orlando in 1995. Seven educators, five of whom had been principals in other schools, were determined to create a school committed to the concept that a rigorous academic education could only be enhanced and become stronger if the arts were an integral part of the core academic curriculum.

We chose a downtown location for a purpose. We wanted the students to take advantage of the cultural facilities available in the area. The Orlando Opera Company, The Orlando Southern Ballet, and the Orlando Sentinel Newspaper were within walking distance. The main library, the courthouse, the Bob Carr Performing Arts Center, and the amphitheater of Lake Eola were minutes away by car. To ensure a strong connection to the programs these places offered, we engaged Robin Jensen, Director of Education for The Orlando Opera Company, and Eliza Harwood of the Orlando Southern Ballet as our music and dance directors.

The first year of operation there was commitment, but no money. Our director, Morris Sorin, had been Superintendent of Schools in a suburb of Ohio and understood what it took to build a school. To him, *building* literally meant "building," so that we would feel ownership and commitment from the start. In addition to developing a curriculum, we learned how to pour concrete and lay tile. Each of us worked without pay for the full year, serving as teachers and custodians so that our "new school" could survive. Survive we did, and by the second year the community began to take notice of us and our arts-infused curriculum. Enrollment grew to 150 students, and we were able to purchase a large piece of property and convert the houses on it into our preschool through eighth-grade classrooms.

In our second year at The New School we at last had time for a second kind of building—the curriculum. We wanted to help the new teachers who had joined our middle school staff understand that history could be taught in a culture-centered way in addition to the traditional political-centered way. We remembered clearly a PBS series, *The Age of Reason*, which explored the period through its art, showing how the statues and paintings depicted mankind with smiles. We wanted to involve these new teachers in an intense interdisciplinary study of history so that they could understand how history and arts are one. To do this, we knew we should begin with a period where history and culture could not be separated. We chose a renaissance in our country: the Harlem Renaissance of the 1920s.

In order to make any interdisciplinary teaching and learning effective, we had to work as a team. From our first meeting with the entire staff, which had grown to seventeen, Morrie charged all of us with the sense that we were going to help the children to create a walk back in time. He urged us to think clearly about the concept of renaissance and how it played out in Harlem. What did we want the children to understand? Etty Baru, who heads the art department, volunteered to help the students research the art and artists of the period. Kathy Williams, the social studies teacher, would help us put the period of the Harlem Renaissance into a world context, as opposed to approaching the era as an isolated piece of history.

Each teacher chose a specific responsibility: Etty would focus on art; Eliza Harwood of the Orlando Southern Ballet would research dance; Robin Jensen would bring her work as Director of Education for the Orlando Opera Company's presentation of *Soul of America* into our classrooms; Morrie would reach into the community to find guest speakers; Kathy Williams kept the historical focus; and I would use the language arts classroom to explore writing and human relationships during the Harlem Renaissance. I would also attempt to tie all our areas together in order to help the students think about the Harlem Renaissance as a whole (e.g., how the mood on Wall Street might influence social habits within our culture or how writers influenced politics).

We met over lunch on a biweekly basis to ensure that we all kept our focus and tapped into each other's energy and resourcefulness. Those meetings were crucial in determining time schedules for the overall project and to adjust, readjust, and adjust again our various classroom schedules. Later, as work progressed, science teachers and elementary teachers kept their students informed about our progress and frequently brought the "little ones" to the upper grade building to watch when we began to add music and dance to our study.

We were clear: this work wasn't to be done as a middle school social studies or language arts project, but rather as a whole school effort. A teacher in any class understands that he or she is a teacher and role model for the kindergarten and the eighth grade at the same time. Middle school students work at lunch and recess time with prekindergarten students.

We saw the project as a living demonstration of how the arts affect nearly everything that we do at the school. We are convinced they heighten, not detract from, a rigorous academic program. Yes, we were going to study a relatively short, but tremendously vital, time in our history. But we were also going to explore a second, larger goal: how to research anything. We promised ourselves that by the time we had completed our Harlem Renaissance project, our students would be able to take any topic, sift through all kinds of information, and bring meaning to it. We also vowed that students would create a product—perhaps a joint book—that showed their understanding. That was before we realized how far-reaching an integrated approach could become.

With that, Annie Sullivan's question became our question, too. How would we present a project on the Harlem Renaissance to a group of 99 percent white children in Central Florida? How could we make it important? How could we make it meaningful?

The Entry Point

To understand the importance of the Harlem Renaissance, we wanted the students to care about the history of the people who eventually moved to Harlem. But this was a single school year in the lives of middle schoolers, a single unit in which to incorporate hundreds of years of history. We decided that if the students could care about and connect with one man's history, we could get further than we could through dozens of history lectures.

The study of history, for most children, is a study of people far away and unrelated to their experience. I decided to use the television series *Roots* as our vehicle. If the students could identify with one man, Kunte Kinte, and his family's struggles, I reasoned, then we could begin to teach the meaning of renaissance in Harlem. If the students could care about one human being, could relate to his suffering, to the forced severance of ties to his family, then the struggle of a people might better be understood. The response to the series was what we had hoped for. Students were shocked. Some cried. Some were angry. Many were ashamed. Most were silent and focused when they watched the tapes, and full of questions each time a chapter ended.

As students watched each unfolding episode, Kathy Williams began to outline history through World War I. This allowed students to see the course of slavery from its earliest beginnings, and start to understand the economic and political purposes for its existence. Each time Kunte Kinte and his growing family moved into a new time period, Kathy explored the history so that the students could continue to imagine real people experiencing real events.

I asked the students to respond in their journals to each new piece of history they saw or read about. The purpose, I explained, was to keep a diary of their thinking, their questions, their feelings, their understandings as a record of how they changed with each new piece of information. The following are excerpts from those early journal entries:

Why did we have to capture innocent Africans and use them for things that we were too lazy to do? We probably destroyed, if not had a powerful effect on, their culture. My ancestors took away whatever dignity those Africans had. To think people wonder why blacks and whites have had problems with each other for so long. We started it; we took them away from their home. We brought them here to America and used them for no reason at all. For once, I am ashamed of who I am. I am ashamed to be white.

Jenni Haygood

Elissa, our class poet, when angered, would always respond in some poetic form. She wept when she saw the portrayal of beatings of the slaves and left this poem by my books:

If we were all born colorless
with silence in our hearts
to die
without a dream
to cloud our vision
to see
but not believe
the faces of our lives
understanding only
how different we are
and how alike
we could have been
would there be
a line
and would there be
a silence
pretending to be hidden
in our skin?
we will not die within our wall
we were not born apart
we were all born colorless
with silence
in our hearts.

Elissa Caffery, Grade 8

All Research Starts with a Question

Typically in schools, reports or research projects have titles such as: "China" or "Florida" or "Greece." Such reports are born directly from encyclopedias and copy machines. We didn't want this. We wanted students to behave as real researchers by learning to ask intelligent, pointed questions. In the language arts classes we told students that we were going to begin a unit that would allow them to explore history, do research, work as a team, and write a book. Write a book? That got their attention. This was to be no ordinary project. They sat up.

I asked the students if anyone had heard of a period of American history referred to as the Harlem Renaissance. As I expected, no one had. And so we began. I asked the students to write ten questions that would be so probing that, if answered, the students would be experts on the Harlem Renaissance. To begin I asked: "What does it mean to be known as an expert on a subject?" The hands shot up.

MIA PEROVETZ: You've got to know a lot about the subject.

ANDREA BOHMER: You've got to know everything about the subject!

ELISSA CAFFERY: It depends on whether you are going to become a
   competent expert. Then you've got to know everything.

"What does a person have to do to become that expert?" I repeated.
   Jenni Haygood said, "Read a lot."
   Cash Blodgett said, "It depends on what you want to become an expert on."
   "On cancer, on World War II, on growing roses, on the perfect sneaker! What does any researcher have to do?" I asked. Silence . . . and then, Elissa Caffery said, "You have to ask some questions."

Then, of course, we had to ask questions about questions. What are the different kinds of questions you can ask? When are yes/no questions exactly what you need? When do they keep you from learning what you need to know? What counts as an open-ended question? What are probing questions? These were the hard ones, students decided, the ones that often did not have yes or no answers. What kinds of questions must the cancer researcher ask? What kinds of questions must the filmmaker ask? What about the genealogist? The criminologist? And what about an historian?

We experimented with changing questions from dead-ended yes and no inquiries into ones that asked for deeper knowledge and understanding. We decided that the kinds of questions that were asked would determine what answers were the best, and therefore, who the best experts were.

ALICE MAGUIRE: What does the word "renaissance" mean?

DANIEL GABRIEL: That's important, but we can get more information to become experts if we rephrase that to say, "What is a renaissance?"

CASH BLODGETT: What was the Harlem Renaissance?

ANDREA BOHMER: Couldn't we say, "What was the significance of the Harlem Renaissance?" and get the same answer, but more? Who were the important people in the Harlem Renaissance?

JAMES COOLE: That would give us names, but if we said, "What role did each major player in the Harlem Renaissance have?" we would get their contributions to the renaissance in a pointed way as well.

By learning to form questions, the students began to take an active role in the research process.

EMILY BENNER: Did you notice that every time we start a question with *did* all we get are yes and no answers? It's cool that when you add the word *how* before *did* you get smarter questions.

It would be misleading to say that after these initial questions were formed, the project was easy. However, learning how to frame them was an extremely important moment in helping to make the work ahead easier.

Emily's observation that changing the question word afforded greater depth in both the search and possible answers within that search and was pivotal in the students' understanding of how to ask a good question. One question, for example, was expressed first as "Did the Harlem Renaissance influence the world outside Harlem?" After the question exercise several of the students responded immediately that by placing *how* before *did* the question became huge: How did the Harlem Renaissance influence the world outside?

We pooled our questions: When did the Harlem Renaissance start? Why did it stop? Why did it start? How did it start? Who organized it? What is a renaissance? Why was it called the Harlem Renaissance? Why was the term renaissance attached to this period?

What things went on during the Harlem Renaissance? Who were the major figures of the time for the Harlem Renaissance? How did each major figure contribute to the Harlem Renaissance? What was going on in the world at the time of the Harlem Renaissance? What did *we* get from the Harlem Renaissance?

What was the significance of the Harlem Renaissance? What were the goals of the people in the Harlem Renaissance? What happened in the world to separate the black and white community? How did the Harlem Renaissance influence the world outside Harlem?

There Is No Output If There Is No Input

We started the students on their search by organizing a list of the important topics/personalities they might need to explore. Since our school emphasizes the importance of multiple intelligences, we organized the list in ways that might initially attract students to their areas of interest. As we were to see later, for some, their early choices and interests were to change dramatically.

We also gave each student a spiral notebook that contained a street map of Harlem, a succinct list on how to cite resources in a bibliography, a time line of major events from 1919 to 1930, and the following chart:

Harlem Renaissance: The Important Players 1919-1930
Add to this list as you do your research.
- Writers/Musicians/Artists
- Photographers/Intellectuals
- Thinkers/Leaders/Periodicals/Actors/World Events
- People/Places of interest

Claude McKay	Wallace Thurman
Countee Cullen	Duke Ellington
Jean Toomer	Cab Calloway
Langston Hughes	Louis Armstrong
Zora Neale Hurston	Eubie Blake
Jessie Fauset	Fats Waller
Charles Johnson	Bojangles Robinson
James Weldon Johnson	Florence Mills
Arna Bontemps	Bessie Smith
Walter White	Ethel Waters
Caspar Holstein	Roland Hayes
Rudolph Fisher	W.C. Handy

Josephine Baker	Charles Gilpin
Fletcher Henderson	Lindbergh's Flight
Alberta Hunter	Babe Ruth Scores
Augusta Savage	Ku Klux Klan
Richard Barthe	Scopes Monkey Trial
Charles Alston	Influenza Epidemic
Miguel Covarrubias	Russian Revolution
Archibald Motley	Apartheid
Meta Fuller	Movies-Talkies
Palmer Hayden	Stock Market Crash
William Johnson	F. Scott Fitzgerald
Philip Van Der Zee	Georgia O'Keeffe
W. E. B. Du Bois	Ernest Hemingway
Alain Locke	George Gershwin
Marcus Garvey	Eugene O'Neill
Jessie Fauset	Cotton Club
Carl Van Vechten	Apollo Theater
The Crisis	135th St. Library
Opportunity	Savoy Ballroom
New York Age	Tree of Hope
Negro World	A'Lelia Walker
The Challenge	The Talented Tenth
The Messenger	Aaron Douglas
The Emancipator	Paul Robeson

The Book Company and the Museum Company Are Formed

One day, the younger classes in the school were at the Orange County Historical Museum where Michele Alexander had begun courses for students on "museuming." In daylong minicourses, she would teach students how a museum operates, give hands-on experiences, and invite students to create a museum exhibit. Jaine LaFay, the fourth-grade teacher, mentioned to Ms. Alexander that our middle school students were studying the Harlem Renaissance.

Jaine asked her if she might be interested in giving our students a minicourse on Florida of the 1920s. Not only was she interested in giving a course, Ms. Alexander had been looking for ways to involve students of Orlando in a project that would allow them space in the museum to create their own exhibits. "Why not use your research and work for your book to create an exhibit that the museum would house and promote?" she suggested. I thought this would be a wonderful way to expand the information students had gathered and give those who preferred to show their information graphically a chance to do so.

Michele arranged for meetings with Morrie, Barry Snyder, the museum exhibits director, and Kerrie Kennedy, the museum exhibits curator, so that everyone would understand the concepts that the school was trying to develop and see how the museum could contribute to that. Michele would give the students a workshop on the realities of museum visitors who tend to stop by each exhibit for no more than twenty seconds. Barry Snyder offered to show the students how to set up an exhibit artistically and to take them into his workshop to use his materials to create the visual effects they wanted. Kerrie Kennedy was preparing a presentation on the Harlem Renaissance for the "Second Sunday Series" that would take place in February. What luck! She agreed to give her perspective as an African American on the role of the Harlem Renaissance.

Now we were doing two projects at the same time. The museum project would use the same information as the book project. Why not? It could give the students an audience for their work and their book. The students were delighted. Now two companies would be formed, a book company and a museum company.

The next step was to let the students choose which topics they wanted to explore and to define roles and responsibilities. Long discussions followed about what it takes to create a book and the role of researchers, writers, editors, reviewers, illustrators, and interpreters of information that had been researched. A study of the Harlem Renaissance is a study of history, literature, art, and music. We knew this and we knew that we must find a way for students to get to know the work of the major artists, writers, and musicians of the period. Why not have the students include a live presentation as part of their museum exhibit?

It was time to call in Robin Jensen of the Opera Company and Eliza Harwood, the primary Dance Coordinator for the Southern Ballet, our dance teacher. We met with Etty Baru and Morrie and brainstormed about the Charleston, Duke Ellington, the Cotton Club, and what our students might be able to do. Visions of students' artwork and essays and a line of them doing the Charleston loomed large. Robin talked about introducing Ellington's work to those who wanted to sing. And, of course, I talked about Langston Hughes and the wealth of poetry we could explore.

No matter how grand our scheme became, Morrie encouraged us to think even bigger. It was ambitious. These were eleven- to fourteen-year-old children, after all. Good research on a book was a large project. It was bold to think the art that Etty Baru and the students might create could possibly be museum quality. Could these children learn the Charleston and sing songs from the era worthy of public presentation, too? We hesitated. Morrie said, "Do it! It will be fun and exhausting. But let's do it!"

It was time to inform the parents about our plans. We sent out a letter describing the project. In closing, we asked for their help:

> I have read the preceding page about the research project on the Harlem Renaissance. These are the questions or comments I have about the project:
>
> _____
>
> _____
>
> _____
>
> I have or know the following resources that might be helpful to the students in their course of study:
>
> _____
>
> _____
>
> _____
>
> I know the following people who could serve as resources to community sessions that will discuss the Harlem Renaissance:
>
> _____
>
> _____
>
> _____

Most parents who responded did so favorably. Several had contacts in the community who might serve as resources for us. There was a drummer, Panama Francis, who had lived and worked in Harlem and Jack Schiffman, whose father owned the Apollo Theater. Alton Lathrop, a dancer and organizer of the Zora Neale Hurston Festival in Eatonville, Florida, might be able to help Eliza with dance.

Only one parent presented an obstacle. "Why," she wrote, "would you want to waste the time of a group of middle-class white students in studying something as remote to their lives as the Harlem Renaissance?" That question was irritating and important. Why teach any history? All history is initially remote to most middle schoolers. It is precisely the irritating question, though, that is important. It keeps you focused and forces you to question where you are going and why. We kept that question in front of us until the very end of our project. But it was not the only time during our work that it was to be asked.

We felt assigning a large project was fine for the high school classroom. But for middle school students, learning how to conduct the process was important. They needed experience with the day-to-day work of gathering information, sorting, classifying, discarding, and reworking pieces of the project. It was important that we be there every step of the way to work with the students as they learned. When they were done, we wanted them to be able to take this experience and transfer it to any other piece of research they encountered.

We prepared the first step of organization for the students: spiral notebooks dedicated to the Harlem Renaissance work. All notes, comments, questions, plans, addresses, lists, and contacts were to be placed into this one depository, giving little chance for the disorganized to misplace note cards or handouts. We had told the students *not* to take notes when they read. We wanted to rid them of the usual copying from texts that takes place when reports are written. Instead, once or twice a week during class, students were asked to take twenty minutes and write down everything they knew about the person or subject they were studying. No books were permitted to be open. Students asked if they might open a book to verify information. We relented.

To build students' background information we showed videos: *America, A Look Back: The Jazz Age* from Time-Life Video; *America's Music: Blues* from Bennett Video Group; *James Weldon Johnson* from Aims Multimedia; *This Fabulous Century: 1920-1930* from Time-Life

Video; *The Twenties: From Illusion to Disillusion* from Films for the Humanities and Sciences; *Witness to History: The Roaring Twenties* from Guidance Associates Video.

Video viewing was not a time for the students to sit back, relax, and enjoy passive entertainment. Before each video was presented we formulated questions that we hoped the video presentation might answer. After each video, we talked about which questions were addressed, which still needed to be answered, and what parts of the presentation raised still further questions. These lists served as information and hypotheses from which to build a thesis about the decade. Students can quickly learn to answer the traditional who, what, where, when, and why questions. What poses tremendous difficulty is the question "All right, you can give me all this information about the person or event, but how is this significant to the decade?"

For example, before viewing *The Twenties: From Illusion to Disillusion*, I asked students what we had already learned about the 1920s. We created lists that included factual information, suppositions, and questions. In this way, the video would confirm, deny, or alter the information we were working with and raise new questions for us.

We taught the same kinds of lessons about listening. We listened to the music of Bessie Smith, Eubie Blake, Louis Armstrong, and Duke Ellington. When I played the Zora Neale Hurston tapes, the students were asked to visualize from her graphic detail what the people looked like, what the neighborhood might have provided. I asked them to draw pictures of her descriptions and to act out the scenes she verbally painted in order to encourage making meaning of the scenes. I continually asked, "What is she trying to make us see? Feel? Know?" And most important "What are we as a reading audience to infer from her descriptions?"

Doing research is hard work and takes planning. No moment is too small or too apparently "natural" or easy to ignore. Even something as apparently simple as brainstorming deserves teaching and interaction. For instance, where can you find information?

ALLISON GREENE: The library.
MIA PEROVETZ: From the poetry itself.
BRANDON ANDREWS: The Internet.

ALICE MAGUIRE: Maybe there are people still alive who could come and
   talk to us.
EMILY BENNER: Harlem!

Students formed new subgroups from which to gather information to
report back to the group. Five students searched for Internet addresses.
James searched for graphics without copyright problems. We have a
large screen monitor for our classroom computer, and the group of five
began to give basic instructions on web searches to those students who
were new on the Internet. The Net-Noir was an excellent place to begin,
they decided. This "Black Network" is designed to be an interactive
online community that is dedicated to Black cultural values in its exploration of people and culture, news, business, and politics.

   Long ago I had learned that if I wanted my students to write well I
had to read to them, read a great deal, and read just before they wrote.
I started reading poetry to the classes—not analyzing, not testing, not
assigning worksheets or vocabulary lists. The focus was on the words,
and what they might have meant spoken during the 1920s. I read
Langston Hughes and Countee Cullen and Claude McKay. What did
Mr. Hughes' voice sound like? They guessed; they tried it out aloud.
Then I showed a video of the life of Langston Hughes and we heard his
voice. Brandon exclaimed, "Oh, God! He sounds like us. I thought he
would sound like a rap artist."

   Many of the boys were surprised that they were responding to poetry. They liked the anger and they liked the love. The words of the poets
started to appear in letters to girlfriends. One student, as he often did,
left a trail of his work behind him. I checked to see if the folded papers
were work he needed for his next class. To my surprise I found a letter
to his girlfriend with the words of Langston Hughes not in quotes:

   Dear _____,
   I love the soft wind's sighing before the dawn's gray light. I love
   the deepness of the blue, in my Lord's heaven above. But better
   than all these things I think I love my lady love. Call me tonight
   before 8:30 p.m.
   Yours in love,
   Your teddy bear

Poetry was no longer girl stuff.

Andrea Bohmer became the person to ask about Langston Hughes and Countee Cullen. She and Mia would sit at lunch time reciting their works. Andrea wrote in her journal:

> This experience put the past and even the present into perspective. The poetry stole my heart. I could relate so well to the work. It took me to the midnight place with paper and pen in hand. While the rest of the world sleeps, my soul is released through the ink of my pen. I could envision the poets and thinkers like Langston Hughes, Countee Cullen and W. E. B. Dubois doing the same as I. Sitting alone in a silent room where the only sound was the faint scratching between the point of my pen and the smooth paper, the only light comes from the small desk lamp to the right. This poetry really hit home and a place I know.

Alice found out about The Schomburg Center for Research in Black Culture in New York City. It was time to learn how to use the telephone for information. She used Morrie's office and set up shop. Alice spoke to people from archives, graphics, and history. They told her names to include if she wanted to discuss art: Aaron Douglas, Meta Warrick Fuller, Palmer Hayden, and James Van Der Zee. She asked where they were located . . . EXACTLY . . . and we smiled at her intensity. This was Orlando. Why did she care where the Center was?

We needed to stop for Winter Break. Everyone was to spend at least two hours in the library during the two-week break gathering books and information. That was a large expectation for a group of students on vacation. But they had begun to take ownership of the project and they produced. Books from libraries and bookstores started to appear. We cleared an entire six-shelf bookcase and dedicated it the Harlem Renaissance. It started to fill up.

Anna made her way to the University of Central Florida and brought back sheet music of Duke Ellington's work. Robin Jensen was delighted. This would help them for their live museum performance. They listened to thirty of Ellington's songs and chose to study "Mood Indigo" and "It Don't Mean a Thing (If It Ain't Got That Swing)."

Alton Lathrop patiently taught students snake hip movements. He explained how waiters might have incorporated the dance movements as they waited tables in restaurants. He encouraged the boys to dance, the teachers to dance, until the entire assembly area was filled with the rhythm and sounds of the twenties. The poetry, the music, the words, the dance all began to take the students back in time to live the culture of the 1920s. Mastering the steps to the dances became important. Singing in the mood of the sadness of "Mood Indigo" and switching to the joy of "It Don't Mean a Thing" gave the students a sense of ownership of the music. The songs, the music, the poetry became their favorite pieces.

All the students had heard of the Charleston. Alton helped Eliza Harwood stage the Charleston scene with the students. "Who wants to learn the Charleston?" she asked. The hands flew in the air. "Who would like to show the world the Charleston belongs to all times?" More hands flying. Everyone wanted to learn the dance; the girls wanted to be flappers.

Elissa had discovered David Levering Lewis' *When Harlem Was in Vogue* and read to us from *The Portable Harlem Renaissance Reader*. She began to recite poetry in the hallway. Mia followed suit. Keely brought back information from an event she attended honoring W. E. B. Dubois in celebration of Black History Month and an adjunct to the annual "Zora!" Festival in Eatonville, Florida.

Alice hadn't gone to any of the local libraries. She had vacationed in upstate New York and had convinced her parents to take her to the Schomburg Center. She brought us back photographs of Zora Neale Hurston, Claude McKay, Langston Hughes, and a calendar of the work of James Van Der Zee.

An additional organizational page was added to the spiral notebook each student was required to keep. It read: Possible sources to help me complete my job. Be certain to get the name, addresses, and telephone numbers for these sources. Keep your lists neat.

Kristen fell in love with the sound of Zora Neale Hurston's words. She and Emily began to debate which source was right, the one that said that Hurston was born in Eatonville, Florida, or the one that said she was born in Alabama. It was important to them to know the truth. Mia, Andrea, and Nourah worried about the same problem when they encountered different information about Countee Cullen's family life. Why were they so bothered by the inconsistencies? They were stuck with the idea that if it is written in a book, it must be true.

This was a wonderful experience because it allowed us to explore how researchers might disagree and what the students, as newer researchers, need to do when they encounter conflicting information. The phrase "the book said so" became less important.

In the midst of all of this, we realized that we had a large lesson to teach. We had already talked with the students about understanding the significance of events, but we didn't appreciate how hard this was for them to understand. The students had been used to writing inter-mediate grade-type biographies that usually produced pink-bow-bound journals of facts. The students had not made the transition to understanding or looking for the reasons we remember famous people or their significance to our world.

We spent the next full week talking about the people we were read-ing about and making lists about "their significance." This concept turned out to be the hardest one of all to teach in the entire project. This was translated into the classroom as: "Many people were born in 1891 and died in 1960. Why do we remember Zora Neale Hurston who was born and died on those dates? Why do we care?"

It was not easy. James Weldon Johnson died when his car was hit by a train. Dramatic, unusual, and true, we acknowledged, but do we remember him because he was hit by a train? And Claude McKay died of heart failure. They were impressed with the event of death! We became more forceful. We outright banned birth, school, marriage, and death from the lists for the time being. For the purposes of these exer-cises, students were limited to giving two pieces of information—and they must be the most important information one should know. Slowly, our forcefulness and iron rules began to work.

The Experts Arrive

The yearly Zora Neale Hurston festival, "Zora!," was on. Groups of stu-dents went to the museum in her honor and listened to others talk about her. They began referring to her as Zora, not in disrespect, quite the contrary. It was because they began to feel close to her work. Ryan Tanner wrote in his journal:

When I was researching Zora Neale Hurston and writing about

her, I did not really know how important she really was. But when we went to the Zora Neale Hurston Festival, I saw an exhibit on her, all the things in memory of her, and all the people who put on the festival who are devoted to her and her memory. I saw that she is an important part of our history and African American history.

Morrie organized an impressive schedule of local residents who lived during or knew about the Harlem Renaissance. If these students were going to write well, we wanted them to have solid information. David Panama Francis came to talk about jazz in Harlem as he remembered it during the Renaissance. He told them that the term *jazz* had initially been a derogatory term. He played his drums and explained to the students the reasons why he thought jazz was no longer what it used to be. "The bands and the drummers no longer use the bass drum. The bass drum is the heartbeat of jazz," he said as he beat his chest. "Jazz no longer has a heart." Drumbeats ruled in the classrooms. Jack Schiffman, whose father had owned the Apollo Theater, shared his stories about all the famous people who had appeared at the theatre. He knew Louis Armstrong and Josephine Baker. He told about how he cried the first time that he heard the lyrics to the song written by Fats Waller "What Did I Do to Be So Black and Blue?" This impressed the students. They asked questions and looked for more books.

Performance as Understanding

Robin Jensen began to put the finishing touches on her Opera Company's Soul of America series. Singers, storytellers, and actors from the black community would gather to perform works that included those by the writers we were studying. She asked if perhaps some of our students would like to be a part of the show opener by reciting some of the poetry they had studied.

We called a lunch meeting, which was open to everyone who might want to recite or read from the poetry they had explored. Although we had expected six or seven students, those most prone to revealing poetic souls, twenty-two students, boys and girls, came with books in hand ready to read. Student could recite as many poems as they wanted.

Most chose one or two. Mia chose nine. Fourteen eventually made the commitment to learn the poetry by heart and come for three different performances at the Opera Company over a weekend.

A field trip to the Orange County Historical Museum, led by Michele Alexander, provided a hands-on workshop that gave the students the feel for writing, in no more than thirty words, the most important information about an artifact. This was an invaluable lesson in learning how to summarize a main idea for museum visitors. How do you capture the essence of a person, an event, an interaction in thirty meaningful words? Michele explained how the significance of a person, event, or topic is crucial to the heart of an exhibit. Students were surprised to hear that museum staff members were used to spending months to prepare an exhibit while visitors might spend no more than twenty seconds' attention to any given site.

Barry Snyder, Director of Exhibits, took fifteen students into his workshop to give them another hands-on experience in the exhibit display. After coming to school and seeing the kinds of work the students were beginning to produce, he allotted a portion of the first floor of the museum for their monthlong exhibit. He taught them how to capture the attention of a roving museum visitor by adding color and texture to help someone to pay attention.

Kerrie Kennedy, Collection Curator of the museum, came to school to talk about collecting, museum display, and the Harlem Renaissance. Students wanted to impress her with their knowledge of poetry and history. They began telling her of the things they had learned and studied. She looked unimpressed and folded her arms against her chest. Kennedy provided the toughest question of all for these mostly white students. Ms. Kennedy is an African American and she simply asked, "Why should I care what *you* think about the Harlem Renaissance? Maybe your presentation of poetry will offend me or others from my community. Be prepared for people to walk out on you." There was stunned silence. The students were hurt. Again the tough and more-than-irritating question appeared doubting the study of black history by white students.

Mia had read in-depth biographies of Countee Cullen and Langston Hughes and memorized dozens of their poems. She had just written a response to reading Countee Cullen:

"Yet do I marvel at a curious thing
To make a poet black and bid him sing." —Countee Cullen

This is one of my favorite lines spoken by a desperate man. A man of dreams trying to survive in such a society, he spoke for me. As I read his poems, I could feel my pain releasing through his words. I may not have experienced what Countee Cullen experienced, as I am white. But, when I say his poems I am humbled and feel that I have been granted a special privilege to stand on a stage and speak for such a man. This project has opened another door in my life.

Mia boldly raised her hand. We waited.

"Countee Cullen and Langston Hughes wanted to be recognized as poets, not black poets. If you do not allow white students to feel close to and accept and cherish their words, then you do not honor them."

Elissa added, "What happened during the Harlem Renaissance should be important to all America. By isolating the events and allowing it to be shared only in the African American community you diminish its importance."

It sounded good, but whether it made an impression on our tough critic or not was still questionable. Ms. Kennedy just quietly laughed.

Writing Begins

Artwork began to take shape. Etty Baru introduced the students to the jigsaw and watercolor so that they might create three-dimensional pieces or soft fluid paintings. Etty, Jordan Probst, and Kristen Bautz experimented with some of the techniques for three-dimensional expression that the students had learned at the museum with Barry Snyder. How could the poetry being studied be represented best? They needed to work at interpretation of the written piece in order to transform it to a different medium.

Leah Stein chose to bring the work of Langston Hughes to life in the art room. She chose to illustrate her poem "Island" and wrote in her journal:

After looking at my piece, some of you may ask why I drew a "stick figure," as the person who is narrating the poem. The stick figure represents a faceless person with no past who can be black or white, male or female. The faraway island represents something that you are reaching for but it is not within your grasp. I suppose in this poem Langston Hughes was portraying a person, probably an African American, who was on the edge of society, pleading with the cold, bland faces of those high in society.

Jasimine Thompson used watercolor to rough draft an art piece of two black and white musicians without eyes. This reflected her view that during the Harlem Renaissance musicians didn't see color. Her piece was chosen for the cover of *Central Florida Family* Magazine's focus on teaching history through the arts. But Jasimine was most impressed by the work of photographer James Van Der Zee. She responded to his work in her journal:

> James Van Der Zee's work has this mysterious quality about it. He portrays Blacks to be a proud race. His work makes you forget the strife and the routine of life. He could make a person who was so troubled inside seem full of life.
>
> He shows Blacks at their finest. James Van Der Zee tried to focus on the positive as opposed to the negative. The photographs all have this arrogance about them that seems to say, "We're Black, but we sure as heck are living it up!"
>
> It's possible that because of the environment that James Van Der Zee was forced to live in, he was exposed to different aspects of life, causing him to think in a different way. Aaron Douglas' environment might have consisted of rich storytelling and folk tales which influenced his art.

Cash Blodgett was a quiet boy who loved art and reading. But I hadn't heard much from him about his responses to art, literature, and the Harlem Renaissance. One afternoon I told him so, and he said, "I'll put it in a letter to you tomorrow." The next day I found this response in his journal:

> The art of the Harlem Renaissance was often overlooked by people focusing on the dance, music, and literature of the era. However, that is not to say that the art was not creative, interest-

ing, and beautiful. With the help of influential people such as William Harmon, artists were provided with the chance to exhibit their artwork for the first time.

Many of the artists based their work on African culture and heritage. One such artist was Aaron Douglas. Aaron Douglas not only depicted his people's heritage, but also portrayed the misery of the blacks throughout the years of slavery.

Another strong influence on the Harlem Renaissance art was the lively nights of Harlem with the streets full of music and the nightclubs such as the Savoy playing live jazz for people to dance to throughout the night. Harlem not only offered visions of endless nights of dancing to paint, it also offered something of a more mellow tone: poetry.

The poetry and art of Harlem went together like jigsaw pieces. Some of Aaron Douglas' works told stories that could be compared with the poetry of writers such as Langston Hughes and Countee Cullen.

Renaissance means rebirth. . . . The artists who first fought against the odds of being black and making a career as an artist in a white man's world paved a path for later generations to follow and no longer hesitate to express themselves in any way that they would like.

There were more and more discussions about what needed to be in a book on the Harlem Renaissance. Of course, the writers and musicians were included. But by this time the students understood that the Harlem Renaissance did not occur in a vacuum. History, politics, and economics set the stage. What was going on in the rest of the world? Who were the newsmakers in the 1920s? Lists and more lists were made, revised, and discarded. The Scopes Trial, Ghandi, and the KKK were included.

Groups formed around the various topics and people that were to be included. Everyone to this point had been an information gatherer. It was now time to break up into groups that could function as teams to produce a product. We discussed possible jobs after we explored what roles the following positions might entail: researchers, writers, editors, reviewers, illustrators, graphic designers, and interpreters.

Elissa Caffery was chosen as editor. She and her group met for hours and hours to come up with an outline of information. It was revised each time they hit an information-gathering snag. Some of the artists and writers seemed always to be mentioned in a phrase like: "So and so . . . and others were influential". The students had to wrestle with the problem that little information was given about some figures who were important to the decade. "Jean Toomer and others" became the phrase in class for not being able to find information. Whenever they used this phrase in class we all knew that it expressed their frustration with trying to ferret out information that was not readily available. It captured and conveyed their frustration for finding dead ends. Three days were spent sifting out the themes they wanted to cover in their book. Their final outline looked like this:

Preface
Introduction
Acknowledgments
The World
The Roar of the Twenties
Monkey vs. God
The KKK
Peaceful Resistance
The Influenza Epidemic
The Teapot Dome Scandal
Inventions
Beginnings
Harlem, Capital of the
   Black World
Political Activists
Marcus Garvey
Jessie Fauset
W. E. B. Du Bois
NAACP
Writers
Claude McKay
Countee Cullen

Langston Hughes
Zora Neale Hurston
James Weldon Johnson
Paul Laurence Dunbar
Entertainers and Musicians
Louis Armstrong
Josephine Baker
Bessie Smith
Paul Robeson
Artists
James Van Der Zee
Aaron Douglas
People and Places of Interest
L'Alelia Walker
Alain Locke
Carl Van Vechten
Josh Gibson
The Cotton Club
Savoy Ballroom
The End of the Harlem
   Renaissance
Bibliography

This was an impressive list. But the students had been reading for close to two months and they had, indeed, become quite knowledgeable. A week was set aside for note card work. We got juice and fruit and candy in for the long haul. Blues music played in the background. The boundaries between classrooms had all but vanished. Students moved freely between the social studies class, the language arts class, and the art studio. Because the students had gone through the exercises of writing down lists of the most significant information, and because they had spent so much time recording information that they remembered rather than copied, going back and taking notes was not a difficult task. They knew what they were looking for now. We talked about how to code the cards so that information was easy to find.

At this point those exercises yielded a framework from which to gather information. All facts were not equal. Some were definitely more important than others. The forty-five students working on the book were aged eleven to thirteen. The older ones abstracted more easily and were good influences for the younger ones. The younger students sought out Elissa, whom they considered an excellent writer, and asked her how to express what they wanted to get across.

ANDREA BOHMER: Elissa, help me say this in a good way about Ghandi.
ELISSA *(Gently):* What is it that you would like to tell your audience?
ANDREA: I want to say that this was a man who has changed the
    world, led millions of people, caused uprisings and chaos for law
    enforcers through nonviolence, hunger strikes, and words.
ELISSA: There you just said it. Write it just like that.

We knew that we wanted excellent work. All teachers do. A year earlier Dennie Palmer Wolf had a chance to visit our school and talk to some of the middle schoolers who were practicing for a presentation of *Romeo and Juliet.* Dennie asked the students what they wanted from their performance. They responded that they wanted it to be excellent. "What would that look like?" she asked. "What does excellent look like?" has been part of our litany ever since. What would an excellent piece of writing look like? The students discussed it and came up with the following list:

It would tell what the contributions of the person were (if it was
a person).

It would tell the significance of that contribution—why it was important.

It would tell what role the person or event played in the HR or the world community.

It would be written without comma splices, or run-ons, or fragments.

It would be well-researched and backed up by facts.

What would the title for the book be? Again, we felt Langston Hughes' influence. It was all about a dream, a vision, they decided. After much discussion and voting it was settled. They would create *The Harlem Renaissance, 1919-1930: The People Who Shared the Dream*. And James finally found the photo for the cover that did not cause a copyright problem. It was a group photograph, posed on a Harlem street, that showed a sense of unity and pride.

It was not as simple to get the information back as the editorial team had expected. The editors were relentless, and everyone knew that. The work would be turned in daily. They would appear to haunt those who procrastinated. One crew typed. Another edited. The editors decided to introduce each chapter with a quote or piece of poetry that seemed to capture the mood of the topic.

The writing style and quality varied according to the strengths and age of the writers. Some students wrote better simply because they were older, some because they were talented. But it was important to the team to respect the writer's integrity. Everyone contributed to the pool of information that was included. Elissa's introduction tried to summarize what they had learned, and the students decided to make the introduction to the book a part of the museum exhibit. From the introduction:

In *The Souls of Black Folk,* W. E. B. Du Bois wrote, "The problem of the twentieth century is the problem of the color line." Seventy years later, we can see the prophesy of his words. But, if we examine them closely, we can also see the paradox.

It seems elementary that the censored cannot speak of censorship until after the fact. Similarly, the outcry of African Americans against racism from 1919 to 1929 signals that their situation must have improved somewhat. The mere fact that Du Bois was heard is enough to indicate that the first steps had been taken toward his goal. Indeed they had. During the decade from the end of World War I to the stock market crash, African Americans produced great literature, music, art, dance, and political commentary, and, almost for the first time, it was appreciated by whites. In addition, they called attention to the predicament of colored people. In these ten years, the black culture was reborn. This movement, centered around Harlem, New York, is known as the Harlem Renaissance.

Never since the empires of Africa had such a high level of black culture existed anywhere. The number of great artists, musicians, poets, authors, performers, and political activists active at the time is not only astounding, it also speaks well for the black situation of the time; one not of integration, but of pride and independence.

When discussing the causes of the Harlem Renaissance, the importance of an all-black environment (Harlem) is often overlooked. At that time in history, integration was all but impossible; indeed, as more than a pleasant theory, it was literally unheard-of. Thus, any African American wishing to achieve any level of true esteem must do so among his peers. In any area of America where blacks were a minority, their talent would likely have been crushed, or at best, ignored. But in Harlem, blacks were the majority by the early 1920s. This naturally allowed blacks to gain power and control over the community, as well as partially escape their status of second- and third-class citizens in white areas. Though racism was still quite commonplace, the omnipresent glare of white disapproval, even hatred, was greatly decreased. If blacks were to shine, Harlem was the place.

They did, indeed. As evidenced by the work of such as Langston Hughes, Louis Armstrong, Aaron Douglas, Paul Robeson, and others, their situation was adequate to nurture and expose their talents, and their talents were unparalleled. This book is about them, their situation, and their significance.

Elissa Caffery, Grade 8 Editor

When we completed our project, we asked the students for an evaluation of their experiences. Many of these evaluations were included a section of the book entitled "Young Historians Speak." They talked about their experience as writers and performers, and some addressed the tough question about why they studied this period.

One student wrote:

> One of the reasons it may have been remote to us is because we never had the chance to study the period. Even though it may be a bigger part of African American history, it is also a part of American history. Therefore, we as Americans, have the responsibility to learn about it. However, it is also a big part of American culture. The Renaissance helped to create such legends as Eubie Blake, Cab Calloway, and Louis Armstrong who will live forever. They were and still are a part of our musical history. If we had not taken the time to learn about them, we could not have kept their legends alive by passing them down to the next generation.

Our work took close to five months to complete. The culmination of student work was a museum exhibit and a book. There were days, as Elissa Caffery said, in which we felt that "the project filled the entire universe." Staff and students worked together in an environment that required patience, sharing, and a finely honed sense of humor.

The local community was responsive to the work of the students, both challenging and validating their efforts. The questions that at first lessened our enthusiasm, "Why would you want to waste the time of a group of middle-class white students in studying something as remote to their lives as the Harlem Renaissance?" and "Why should I care what *you* think about the Harlem Renaissance?" proved to be two fine questions indeed. They focused our attention on the importance of the Harlem Renaissance not just as a unit of research study. They taught us to answer that question for any project we might explore.

"Why?" is an appropriate question for all teachers to answer when choosing what to explore with students. By answering the "why" questions the significance of the project became clear. We learned how to explore the historical, social, and economic realities of a time in history, had a glimpse of how a cultural revolution grew, discussed the music, art, and literature of the period, and tried to address how powerfully the arts and politics are related.

What did the students learn from this experience? We hope that it is, in large part, what Elissa's excerpt from the book's preface explains:

[Students] chose their own path to learning: which ever medium they most enjoyed would most likely be the one through which they would most easily and effectively learn. Those students who loved music were the dancers and singers, the ones with a talent for language were writers and editors. Though all the students contributed in some way to the book or the museum exhibit that accompanied it, their roles were not assigned. By working to perfect a carefully choreographed dance routine or memorizing their favorite poem, they learned the period directly, rather than learning about it. It is next to impossible to forget a person or event about which one has written five pages. It is also difficult to forget a period of history to which one has devoted so much time and effort. By using the arts as a way to learn, they made the Harlem Renaissance a part of themselves.

References

Lewis, David Levering. 1979. *When Harlem Was in Vogue*. New York: Oxford University Press.

Frederick, H. 1996. *Zora Neale Hurston Stories*. Audio cassette. New York: Audio Bookshelf.

Videotapes

America, A Look Back: The Jazz Age. 1989. Video recording. Producer: National Broadcasting Company, Inc. Venice, CA: Ambrose Video Publishing, Inc.

America's Music: Blues 1. 1994. Video recording. Director: K. Walton. Venice, CA: Bennett Video Group.

James Weldon Johnson. Video recording. Chatsworth, CA: Aims Multimedia.

The 20s: From Illusion to Disillusion. 1992. Video recording. Princeton, NJ: Films for the Humanities, Inc.

This Fabulous Century: 1920-1930. Video recording. Richmond, VA: Time-Life Education, Inc.

Witness to History. 1990. Video recording. Mount Kisco, NY: Guidance Associates.

Response from a Colleague:
Crossing Boundaries and the Harlem Renaissance Project

Robin Jensen

When I was a student, a long, long time ago, my parents told me that I had to go to school to get a good education. Without a high school or college degree, I would not have the edge that I needed to get ahead in this world. So I went to school and I tried to get comfortable in those old hard wooden desks lined up straight as arrows in five neat rows. I sat with notebook and pen in hand and wrote down every important word they said and hung on to the answers that I thought would please them. But I knew then that I wanted to be a musician or an actress: why know when Millard Fillmore was president? For what a chemistry periodic table? It seemed as easy as two plus two, until, years later, when I was all grown up and working for an opera company. That's when the *four* part came into focus: It's the learning *how* and asking *why* that really matters.

An interdisciplinary project like The New School's Harlem Renaissance is an especially likely place to need that *how* and *why*. Like other projects that blur boundaries and jump barriers, this one led to unexpected places. None of us expected the boys to fall in love with poetry, or for it to be recited in the halls. No one expected more than a few students to try dancing the Charleston. But perhaps the most unexpected piece of the curriculum was the conversation between these overwhelmingly white students and the African Americans who were asked to open up their heritage.

The Unexpected Question

Last year, the New School of Orlando had one African American student enrolled in the middle school, so the topic of the Harlem Renais-

74

sance seemed at least odd when the school called to ask my help. But on my first visit to school, I was surprised to learn that Langston Hughes had become a household name and to hear the students recite his poetry from memory for each other with a real passion for the meaning of the words—making the words their own. It was clear that the students thought of that time simply as an important period in American history. It didn't matter that they had white skin—they found the poetry compelling.

Since I am not an expert on the Harlem Renaissance, I asked a colleague, Alton Lathrop, a local African American dancer and stage director, to assist me in choosing music and choreographing several dances that were to become a part of a museum presentation—one of the culminating events of the project. Alton's response at first was caution, almost disbelief. "You mean they are all white students studying about this?" Only gradually did it make sense to him to let us in on "his" heritage. At first, we both found it jarring to have the majority of performers be young white students. As Alton worked with us on finding the right "stylistic" nuances and personality to make the music and dance as authentic as we could, he began to see the larger purpose of our endeavor. But he and I and the students were all aware that these stylistic factors were a sensitive issue. No one wanted to come off as white children mimicking or making a parody of the black musical dance style.

Orlando has a rich African American heritage. Nearby Eatonville is the home of Zora Neale Hurston and one of the first free black communities in the South. Many of our major artists—opera singers, writers, and musicians—are African American. Panama Francis, a local resident who is also a well-known jazz drummer, visited the school and surprised everyone with an impromptu performance with a jazz band.

When, as a producer, I asked the New School to be a part of the Soul of America performance, I knew we were stepping over boundaries no one had crossed before. Since the beginning, these concerts featured African American performers, composers, and writers. I also knew that at least one other visitor to the school had challenged the appropriateness of the project. So I asked myself, "How would the community embrace the image of young white children performing their favorite poetry and songs from the Harlem Renaissance at what had otherwise been an all-black event?"

The weekend schedule at the Dr. Phillips Center for the Performing Arts included three concerts. As producer, I had a long list of African American performers including professional opera singers, the Bethune College Gospel Singers, the University of Central Florida Jazz Band, a local ethnic dance company, and the Tajiri Arts (an African American children's theatre company). When I approached the opera administration about including the New School students in the performance, I was confronted with the question, "How would the other performers and the audience feel about having white students be a part of the cast for an all African American musical showcase?" In the end, we compromised: the New School students performed prior to the concert, outside the hall.

The students set up a small stage at the entrance to the theatre; from there they recited and performed their favorite poems and songs as the concertgoers waited to enter the performance. At first there were a few feathers ruffled, but as the other performers listened to and saw the enthusiasm and commitment that the New School students threw into their work, they acknowledged that the students were anything but tourists stopping by where they didn't belong. When the students became the audience, they were treated to renditions of their favorite poems set to music by African American composers. When they listened to a classical art song, murmurs filled the seats as they all recognized the poetry.

I don't know whether any of these students had ever been an outsider before. I doubt anyone had ever questioned their entry or suggested that they stay on their own side of the fence. From my hours in school and rehearsal, I know it was disturbing. But being stopped at the border, having to answer for your intentions, and living out the negotiations are lessons that don't come to those who stay in the lines.

Tools for Success: Collaboration, Cooperation, Organization

What I saw, especially working as a "specialist" on the project, was an opportunity for the students to apply and put the pieces of the puzzle together. They also learned how to use the puzzle! In addition to academic studies, the students learned how to ask a question and confidently know where and how to research and compile the information that would bring an answer. They applied organizational skills and worked in situations that mirrored real-life careers. They developed a confidence in themselves to pursue the questions and seek them out in their community. They learned how to be a part of other organizations in their community. Many of us have a dream to write that big book. We have ideas and concepts that we could invent, if only we knew how to begin. The students experienced how to take a concept, an idea, a dream, and make it into reality. They also developed important social skills and learned how to collaborate on a shared vision and goal—all skills that are just as important in education as the academic knowledge acquired.

3

The Art of Observation

The Place of Visual Thinking in Science

Luella Stilley and Dennie Palmer Wolf

Introduction:
Confessions of a Former High School Teacher

It was a hot and bright August day when I moved to Memorial Junior High School (now Memorial Academy for International Baccalaureate Preparation) in San Diego, California, and met my first classes of eighth graders. By the end of our first day together, I knew that only the most minimal science had been available at their elementary schools—an interested teacher here and there might have hatched chicks or grown plants as part of homeroom or for an elective. I know that even in seventh grade science was not a core subject—students only get three short units. Together, my students and I faced responsibility for learning the equivalent of a nine-year stretch of science education—from biology to bibliographies—in one eighth-grade year. It was one of those impossible assignments only a determined teacher and an equally determined set of students would ever dream of taking on.

For me, the answer was not a crash course in science vocabulary or a rushed overview of earth, life, and physical sciences. Instead, I saw my responsibility as twofold: first, I had to engage students who had not had the chance to develop scientific thinking in becoming curious about how scientists investigate a question; second, I had to give them a sharp sense that this kind of careful investigation was worth all the time, methods, and attention it took. I wanted my students to learn to observe—to hone their visual thinking skills much the way a painter does before setting out to paint a still life or a landscape.

It was not going to be easy. Part of the challenge was me. As a secondary-trained teacher with a departmental mindset, I was uneasy about modifying my well-honed methods of teaching, especially if it meant I was going to have to take on the noisy, messy logistics of project work. I knew it was going to be difficult for me to turn to what one of my colleagues calls "cutesy things"—group work, drawing, oral presentations—exactly those activities that my middle school colleagues said would help my students wrestle with big ideas new to them. Frankly, these activities didn't seem like "real work" to me. Perhaps most unnerving of all, I could sense that if I wanted my students to understand why scientific investigation mattered, I might have to leave the safe islands of biology and chemistry for the blurrier territory of interdisciplinary teaching. I knew that being able to draw to scale or consider an object's texture, shape, and size were important tools in science, but I never thought of them as full-fledged partners. And the idea of "giving up" precious science time to construct, write, and draw seemed like an outright waste.

Some would say there is no better or more rewarding place than middle school to take on teaching in an integrated, project-based fashion. The lore is that in a self-contained classroom you are designer, timekeeper, and jury. All of the components are easily accessible—time under your command, all your students in one classroom, the right to mesh subject areas, the possibility of creating assessments that bridge otherwise separate areas, and the chance to see those rare and important moments when students suddenly make connections between disciplines. But, frankly, I didn't believe it. I didn't want to be teaching one of those interdisciplinary mashes where all the subjects are shoehorned in and none is taught with integrity. I was only interested in genuine connections. If I was going to do this, I wanted to be doing worthwhile science at the same time that I was teaching real literacy, good history, or the fine art of observation. I sensed that meant unearthing situations where both the content and the strategies of different subject matters genuinely overlapped. And, as far as I could see, episodes of this kind of partnership didn't exactly grow on trees.

I had one resource I could depend on: my students. They were willing and smart and full of that uncommon alertness and honesty that belongs to many urban students:

Sometimes I wish to sleep one night without worrying who will
be the next person getting assaulted, jumped, or killed. In my
neighborhood there's two stores, one in each street. In these
streets there are all kinds of drug dealers. . . . In front of my
house there's a church for African Americans. Every Sunday and
Wednesdays [we] could hear them sing with their lovely voices.

JoAnne

The good thing about this neighborhood is that they have lots of
places you can go to have fun and lots of pretty places. Well it's
not only because they have pretty places it's also because [there]
are many people that are very sharing and nice to all the people
that ask for help or some money. They give what they have . . .
they give them some tacos because all the people that live in our
neighborhood are mostly Mexican people . . . the people that go
and ask for food they say that it's so good and they thank them
lots of times but our neighborhood people tell them that they can
come every time they want that they will always be waiting for
them to help on what they need.

Patricia

But many of my students' families had never had the opportunity to finish school; they had left their homes in order to ensure that their children
would have educational opportunities they had never known.
Consequently, many of my students were, even as young adolescents,
figuring out the routines and habits of secondary school on their own.
They had transitioned from bilingual classrooms long before they were
ready, so that they were struggling after the nuances of academic
English. And, most pointedly, as young people capable of doing good
science, they had been cut off from the opportunity even to begin. They
had never used a microscope, no one had asked them to collect data, and
no one had ever challenged their explanations by asking for evidence.

In short, if you had told me that today I would be teaching archaeology as the meeting place for the sciences and the humanities to eighth
graders who were science novices, I would never have believed you.

But to get there, I had to become something of a detective. My first
stakeout was the American history course my partner taught. Like

someone tracking a rare species, I set myself this pair of questions: "Where did science play a vital role in the country's history?" and "Where could the outcome have been different if it weren't for science?" One of the first connections I made was between the Civil War and battlefield medicine. Together, my partner-teacher and I tried to give students a picture of the power of science by studying the bacteria that caused so much of the disease that drove the death tolls up. Using the few microscopes we had, we set out to sharpen our visual thinking skills. We examined how invisible the bacteria are to the naked eye and modeled how bacteria spread unless simple sanitation procedures like sterilizing instruments and washing hands are enforced. Even if the unit was not perfect, our enthusiasm cascaded over to students. We learned a lot: about crowding too many activities in, about conducting activities for which we weren't sure what we wanted the students to take away, and especially about the danger of turning science into a sidebar for history. If our purpose was for students to learn to investigate, they had to be asking questions, collecting data, and coming to conclusions—not just revisiting investigations others have already made. We were beginning to understand how to forge genuine partnerships between subjects.

Whatever the difficulties had been in the first round, we had certainly demonstrated the payoff for bothering to investigate. It was clear to my students how research could make a difference. But if I wanted my students to have the thinking skills, methods, and content that would let them thrive in high school science courses, I would have to create a year's worth of linked units that made these bigger outcomes possible.

The Beginnings of a Native American Unit

As I began to rethink my series of units that would couple science and American history, intuition struck. To understand Native American cultures you really have to understand the biomes in which those cultures took shape. Would it be possible to build off of that meeting of biology and history? Could we use the investigative tools of archaeology on the one hand and research strategies in the humanities to build that understanding? Could we rely on visual thinking as a way to complement their reading and other traditional forms of research? I was excited. The partnership between the subjects was elegant, not forced: real archaeologists live and work right at the intersection between history and science. Also, the built-in detective work of archaeology might provide a perfect mix of an engaging approach that still had the integrity of a high-demand search for relevant evidence.

As I planned the unit with my teaching partners, we thought carefully about how it would help our Memorial students reach the very high standards that our cluster of schools and our district were now setting for all students. Consequently, part of our design process was to ensure that the unit would provide a context for applying mathematics and communicating findings clearly in "academic" or "world" English. At the same time, we wanted to keep ahold of several other very important learnings that brought together the worlds of science and history. In creating a road map for our outcomes, this is the contract that we wrote for ourselves.

At the close of this unit students will be able to:

- understand the intricate relationship between Native American tribes and the biomes in which they lived;
- experience the archaeological approach to science;
- understand the impact of the biome on its inhabitants, such as the relationships between the natural markings of plants/animals and their survival rate in the biome in which they live, and the kinds of artifacts a culture living in the biome produces;
- understand similarities and differences between the various Native American tribes and between Native Americans and other cultures;
- understand how contemporary Native American cultures continue to have to adapt to the demands/pressures of the modern world.

When I looked at this list, I felt cautious—or cautious for me, anyway. First, I wanted to do justice to both the biology and the archaeology, even though I had limited equipment, no real artifacts, and no formal training as an archaeologist. Second, both my students and I would have to learn how to enter and understand Native American cultures to which we were all outsiders.

The Native American unit has now matured through three rounds of teaching. In the process, it has grown to have three distinct sections.

First, in the archaeology project, students learn about the science of archaeology and discover some of the methods scientists use to investigate a question. Students also become familiar with the job of an archaeologist by working out which Native American culture could have left behind the array of artifacts in an archaeological "find." Second, in their history and English class, students develop an understanding of different Native American tribal cultures by reading the history and the literature of that tribe, as well as contemporary journalism that discusses Native Americans' efforts to keep their cultures alive in a modern world. Third and finally, in their science classes, students create an archaeological "find" that represents the ecology and culture of the people they have been studying. This includes the construction of a model bone that reflects the specific anatomy and environment of that people. The components of this find are based upon the tribal information learned in both their history and science classes. This find becomes the next year's science classes' archaeological find.

Project Overview

Together my students and I begin with the most basic scientific tools. I don't mean burners and balance scales, but observation, careful measurement, scientific illustration, and the basic ingredients of a lab report. We practice these in the context of simple investigations and demonstrations that allow students to gain a real command of these basic building blocks. In math class, we do much the same. We review (and in some cases learn for the first time) data collection techniques along with graphing skills and key concepts such as mean, median, and mode. Students learn how formulas are developed to reflect basic observed regularities in the natural world. Not incidentally, we also review and practice the collaborative group behaviors that are essential to our joint work.

In history class, we lay the same kind of foundation. There, for instance, students rehearse basic geographical tools of map reading and mapmaking. Similarly, students review note taking, using it as an occasion for pushing comprehension beyond the most literal levels. We also talk about how to translate information into one's own words, rather than copying it out like a robot. For example, we rehearse the how-tos of reading primary source documents, which students can use over and over, no matter what the piece is or when it was written. We start by reading short newspaper articles and move on to reading more complex kinds of pieces. In each case, we read aloud and develop a shared understanding, paragraph by paragraph, working out the meaning of vocabulary in context, establishing when the piece was written, chasing down as many clues as possible, and we discuss how the time period in which it was written is likely to have affected the content. We also discuss who was writing the piece and who the intended audience was, and how that might affect the kinds of information that were included and excluded. Time and again, we return to a basic set of questions such as "Is this account one-sided? Who else, beyond the author, would agree with it? Is there likely to be another point of view?"

The Archaeology Project

The archaeology component of the Native American project was my first chance to show my students that the kind of inquiry they had begun in their history class is a useful way of working on any investigation—even one in science. As we began, I told them they were about to become archaeologists—investigators who take on the challenging work of piecing together how people lived in other times and places: real people, in fact, who rely on visual thinking in their everyday work.

Then each group received its find, a diverse array of artifacts representative of the setting and culture of a particular Native American culture. For example, the find for one tribe (the Chinook peoples) contained a fragment of a simulated human forearm bone, a piece of wood carved into the shape of a bird's head, blueberries, mussel shells, a pinecone and needles, a dried fish head, corn, pumpkin seeds, beans, a wooden bowl, deer droppings, a piece of sea lion skin, a piece of bearskin, birch bark inscribed with symbols, a hunk of wool, and a piece of woolen weaving. Each team of student archaeologists was challenged to use both the artifacts and as much research as they could amass to identify the region and culture from which the find could have originated. Students began by carefully examining, measuring, drawing, and numbering each of the items in their find—just as an archeological team might. They discussed what they thought each of the items was, recording both their information and their hunches into their archaeologist's logbook for later reference. Success at this initial part of the project was crucial. If students engage at this moment, they begin to "buy into" the entire project. Because accuracy is so important in science as well as in archaeology, I urged students to be especially careful in this first step. They took me at my word. For example, one group poring over the Chinook find were, as urban children, particularly puzzled by the deer droppings. But I urged them to view them as evidence and to track down what they might be. They began by eliminating rabbits:

"... they have little round greenish balls."
"That's because you feed them green pellets from the store."
"In the brush they are brown."

Their visual thinking was underway. They surmised that the droppings of other animals, like raccoons, would also be small. They began to talk about what they had learned about the role of buffalo chips in Native American plains cultures, and segued from there to the conclusion that the size of the droppings and the size of the animal were probably correlated. Given the pine needles and cones, as well as the pine bowl, they surmised the droppings had to come from an animal from the coniferous forests, but bigger than a rabbit or raccoon. They eliminated the larger animals like elk, certain that their droppings would be more the size of a buffalo's. They eliminated mountain lions, based on the shapes they had observed in their own cats' droppings. They settled on deer as the most likely candidate. I was amazed. The initial chorus of "yucks" and "ughs" had me believing they would never be able to settle down to investigating this clue. But the detective work of inquiry drew them in.

After the initial investigations, we talked over what students had been able to discover and their relative degrees of hunch and certainty, then each "archaeologist" wrote down his or her initial hypothesis about individual articles. We revisited this process as teams attempted to synthesize their information into hypotheses about which Native American people could have left behind the entire collection of articles in their find. At this early moment in the project, many students chose the Aztec people of Mexico—despite the fact that they knew the project focused on the Native peoples of North America. They wrote what they hoped for or were interested in since many of them have family in that region. While a wish is a long way from a hypothesis, I took these initial hunches as signs of connection, as well as indications that we had important work to do together.

Next the students began their background research. This had two halves: the work we did in history and literature classes, and the investigations of major biomes that took place in their science class. In science, students worked in small groups where they researched each of the biomes and made lists of the plants and animals living in the specific biome. While they didn't especially like doing what they saw as the "dry" part of the research, I argued to them that the information was the stuff of the clues that they would need as archaeologists to make sense of their finds.

The biome research picked up when I asked them to illustrate the plants and animals for each North American biome. But the concept of a biome as a linked community of animals and plants matched to a climate only really came alive at last on a field trip to the San Diego Zoo. There students could at last apply their knowledge as they identified the six biomes we studied and for which we sketched the vegetation and animal life. We were also sticklers for geography. I wanted them to understand how much of culture could be determined by the natural resources and limitations of the physical world in which Native American peoples lived—both then and now. The maps that students drew and divided into biome regions in the history class proved to be essential information in identifying the region that could have hosted a culture leaving behind the artifacts in their find. I was pleased to see them creating visual representations of their understanding and using drawing as more than merely decoration for their report covers, which is often the norm for middle schoolers. In adding their knowledge of biomes and regions to their analyses of their finds, students were able to make educated guesses as to the region and specific ecology that might have given rise to their find.

As students accrued this basic information, I insisted that they organize it, entering it in a grid that would let them use it later in drawing their conclusions. The grid listed candidate Native American cultures on the left side and the inferences they could draw from their finds across the top (e.g., pinecone and needles = conifer forest; mussel shells and sea lion skin = close to ocean). I was trying to make the processes of drawing inferences and making deductions visual and available to the widest possible range of students. This was an important piece of work throughout the unit. I was constantly searching for strategies and devices (like the grid) that would introduce complex thinking process-es to students who had no experience with them—without boring stu-dents whose intuition or earlier schooling had made these processes almost second nature. This search for what lies between assigning workbook pages and simply assuming that everyone understands remains one of the most difficult processes in my teaching.

As a part of our research work, students participated in a field trip to the Museum of Man in Balboa Park. Rather than the usual filing-by glass cases, this was a field trip with a point. I saw it as yet another opportu-nity to address the question of what constitutes evidence and what con-clusions can be drawn from that evidence. With some help, students came to see it as a treasure hunt for more clues. At first, many students chose to draw containers of one kind or another in their notebooks, probably because baskets and jars by far outnumbered any other kind of artifact. We talked over the universal need for storage, especially among peoples who moved from place to place. But then, looking across the many different containers, we discussed what the differences in their materials, structure, and decoration might tell us. We surmised, for instance, that wooden containers may have come from settings in which trees were plentiful, not rare. Pottery jars signaled clay deposits as well as an understanding of how to fire pots. Baskets hinted at grasslands. Students pushed on to wonder if very elaborate baskets signal a culture that was settled, rather than one that moved regularly. From this activi-ty, students returned to their own find with a clearer sense of how to determine the possible significance of their various artifacts.

Next, I wanted students to have a taste of the tools and techniques that scientists and archaeologists develop to help them in their investi-gations. We turned to the example of radiocarbon dating by doing an investigation about half-lives. Each find contained a plaster of paris model of a bone accompanied by its radiocarbon "reading." (These bones and readings had been put together by the "archaeologists" from the previous class. Having to "make up" this data made me long for access to all the genuine artifacts we had seen only days before.) My current students learned how archaeologists use this information to calculate the age of artifacts containing carbon and calculated an approximate date for when the bone's owner died. Next we discussed how, based on identifying the type of bone and data about the proportions in the human body, it would be possible to arrive at the approximate height of the bone's owner. Our next step was for each team to compare their findings to a database that described the characteristic heights and weights of individuals belonging to different Native American cultures. The result: one more very defensible clue as to the identity of the people who could have left their find.

The Native American Experience: Research in History and Literature

Even as we built up our body of clues from the inert remains in each find, I wanted my students to develop a sense for the human lives that were behind the artifacts. We began with a series of short Socratic seminars, each focused on a quotation from a Native American culture that was linked to the biology research we had been conducting.

> We are a part of the Earth and it is part of us. This we know. The earth does not belong to us. We belong to the earth.
>
> *Chief Seattle*

> What is life? It is the flash of a firefly in the night . . . it is the little shadow which runs across the grass and loses itself in the Sunset.
>
> *Crowfoot*

In those seminars we worked on drawing all we could out of each short statement, much as we had been trying to extract all the meaning we could from materials as simple as pine needles or a grass basket. We also did a good deal of writing that built on their work in science. For instance, students read myths from the people they believed to be behind their find and tried to write another myth from that culture, using the clues from their find, the evidence in the myths they had, and ideas drawn from our seminars. Together we read the letter from Chief Seattle to President Pierce, calling for respect for the Native American ways of life, as well as a number of current newspaper articles describing issues in contemporary Native American lives. For instance, we read pieces ranging from accounts of how Native Americans are seeking the return of sacred artifacts from museums to a piece about a Native American student who cannot wear her medicine bag of sacred herbs in school. We also read a collection of articles that described how Native Americans are seeking to keep hold of their cultures even as they lead contemporary lives. One described how tribal courts have sought and won jurisdiction over the sentencing of their young, meting out traditional punishments in place of prison terms.

We talked for a long time about a case in which two adolescents involved in a robbery were banished to remote islands where they will have to live off the land for a year, with nothing but a sleeping bag and tools for cutting wood and gathering food. We also read about Native Americans' efforts to hold on to traditional cures for diseases that affect members of the tribe, even such serious diseases as diabetes. At the close of these discussions, my students wrote a contemporary version of Chief Seattle's letter, based on their insights about Native American peoples' efforts to adapt to biomes that have become radically different from what they once were.

An interesting by-product of all this reading is that students began to comment on the wide variety of Native American names—some immediately recognizable as Indian, others clearly Hispanic, some indistinguishable from Anglo names they know. What seems like a small detail turned out to give my students a clear sense of how Native Americans are a part of many different communities. This was driven home by a visit from one of our counselors, whom all the students think of as Hispanic, but who is Native American. He came to class dressed in his traditional costume and talked with them about his life moving between several cultural worlds—something they are trying to master just as he has.

Pulling Together the Evidence

After all of the research was collected and recorded, students used their grids to try and narrow their findings and reach a conclusion based upon their evidence. In addition, I showed students how they might use Venn diagrams to organize the information in still another way. As I mentioned, each of these was an effort to help students who are just beginning to understand this kind of evidence-based investigation to "see" the patterns in their findings. But legislating insight is not easy. For some students these visual organizers proved invaluable, but for others who do not think in this highly structured mode, it was hard. They simply put some writing in the different compartments. However, in virtually every group, there was someone who grasped how to use these tools. (This left me thinking that perhaps human models—other students who can describe their thought process—more than grids and diagrams, may have the greatest power to open up new ways of thinking about information.) A number of students' early conclusions were incorrect—chiefly because students had used their data selectively or drawn implications that could not really be supported. In each of these cases, I challenged the team to convince me that their find items did indeed support their conclusion. This give-and-take between us helped students to go over their data with a fine-toothed comb, to prepare their evidence, and to hone their persuasive skills.

One example stands out in my memory. In one of my classrooms, two groups concluded that they each had a find from the Pomo peoples. Actually, one find was indicative of the Pomo, while the other drew on the biome and culture of the Paiute. The Paiute lived on the eastern side of the Sierra Nevada, whereas the Pomo lived on the ocean side. So, I challenged the students with the Paiute artifacts to convince me they were from the Pomo culture and geography. This was their rationale:

- The acorns, seeds, and roots proved they were gatherers.
- The piece of woven grass proved they were weavers and that their biome contained grasses.
- Rabbit, squirrel, and deer skins and the fish proved that there was game and water nearby. (They couldn't tell it was a fresh-water trout, not an ocean fish.)
- Corn and beans were available for the Pomo.
- The drawings on the animal skin were of a wickiup, bushes and trees with mountains in the background. (The sketchy drawings didn't show the differences between a more temporary housing unit covered in branches, brush, and mats of the Paiute, and the more stable, larger wickiup covered with tightly woven mats characteristic of the Pomo peoples.)
- The size of their simulated bone indicated Pomo. (It also could have

been Paiute.)

Further, they argued that because the biomes were somewhat the same, the same materials and artifacts were likely to come from each. It was difficult to fault their logic. Moreover, that was not the end of the story. Later, when they were asked to create a find for the following year's class, they researched the fine differences between Pomo and Paiute cultures so that they could include artifacts that were specific to the Paiute, and did not overlap with what might be in a find for the Pomo culture. As a result, they revised the artifacts in their find to contain wool from a mountain sheep and a digging stick useful in that hilly region.

The last activity, writing the archaeologist's report, was extremely important. The students knew that this report was their evidence showing that they understood how an archaeologist builds a case. These final performances made it very clear how demanding the assignment was. Drawing inferences, backing them up from other sources, and synthesizing them into a coherent whole is the work of a lifetime. Daniel's essay arguing that his find indicates the presence of Navaho people demonstrates the challenge of going from possible clues to a conclusion based on evidence:

> The turquoise from our Find may be of religious significance or maybe not. There was no evidence on what religion they had. The only thing is that there were some symbols on the pot. We are studying what those symbols might mean. The turquoise was a neat rock to have for them. They also may have used it for decoration.

Even when a student has begun to master investigative and evidential strategies, there is the additional challenge of pointing out the explicit ties between evidence and conclusions. Part of an essay by Luis makes this clear:

> I am Dr. Luis T . . . archaeologist in charge of the Find which I have called tribe number #05. From the following evidence I have concluded that these people came from the Paiute tribe. I have based my conclusion on the following evidence such as corn, grass, dry grapes, deer droppings, sand, piece of cloth with

deer, sea shells, dry berries, and pottery.

He then writes about the conclusions he can draw from the corn, straw-berries, sand, and cloth. He continues by drawing strong conclusions from the shells in the find:

> There were also five sea shells that were different colors, sizes and shapes, so that means that those sea shells came from a water biome. Since there was no other evidence that this people lived near the ocean that is not the answer. The Great Salt Lake areas have evidence of sea. Another explanation is that they traded them for other objects. These sea shells might have been used for orna-ments, food (meat inside), jewelry and for religious ceremonies.

Luis continues by describing his findings on the bone, saying it comes from a male teenager, about 5'2". But he does not draw the final link to the Paiute peoples. He also draws the conclusion from the deerskin that the people leaving his artifacts may have worn deerskin aprons for modesty. But again there is no explicit tie to why this points to the Paiute culture.

Finally, there is the hard work of wrestling academic English to the ground: getting ahold of all the subtle vocabulary and moves that make the point of sentences clear and the connections between ideas visible. Beatriz has the idea of evidence and the strategy of making the connec-tions explicit, but the English of at least her early drafts does not always stand up to the strength of her thoughts:

> My name is Dr. Beatriz M . . ., I'm the archeologist in charge of the "Find" which I have called tribe 1. The tribe of my find was the Seminole and probably lived in an area of warm and tropical climate.
>
> I based my conclusion on the following evidence that my tribe had:
>
> • Tree crusts, indication of Forests, or land near water, possible indication that my person lived in a deciduous forest. Taiga, *tropical,* and perhaps grass lands. Tree crusts indicates trees and one can find an abundance of trees in a Tropical Biome.
> • Red and green feathers, probably from a parrot; it indicates a Tropical biome. Red and green are very colorful and live in

the rain forest more than any other Biome the birds are colorful in order to camouflage themselves; blend in with the colorful plants.
- Deer skin, is another possible indication of vegetation which
  also supports my recent evidence about my tribe being
  Seminole. Why does the deer indicate vegetation? Well, it's
  because the deer mostly live in forests and highly vegetated
  areas. They need vegetation in order to survive.

Creating a Find

In the third phase of the project, the students created a find to be used
by the following year's teams of young archaeologists. The find was to
be based on all of their expertise and knowledge about their specific
tribe. They created a sampling of the clues that a team of archeologists
might find if they were to excavate a site where the culture that they
studied had once lived, worked, and worshipped. They were now constructing the puzzle from the other side. Together we agreed that every
find needed to include this range of clues:

- plaster model of a forearm bone based on the data about the height
  of people in their tribe;
- plant evidence from the biome where their tribe lived;
- animal evidence from the biome;
- mineral evidence from the biome;
- food evidence from the biome;
- an artifact made from the materials available in the biome (such as
  the wood carving of a bird, or the wooden bowl in the Chinook
  find);
- religious or ceremonial evidence;
- evidence about how the people survived (e.g., whether they were
  hunter-gatherers, farmers, fishers, and so forth);
- two additional artifacts of the group's choosing.

This year as we worked, some very interesting points of discussion
arose. For instance, students insisted that they needed to bring in much
more specific specimens than corn, beans, and squash seeds, since they

had learned that almost all of the Native American tribes have these three foods. Similarly, rabbit and deer were equally well distributed throughout the biomes. They hunted down clues that were much more specific than in previous years: dark fur labeled as being from a black bear; scallop shells; and small totem poles replicas. I was frankly pleased. These discussions told me that my students really grasped the way that strong conclusions were based on specific and distinctive evidence.

Assessing What Was Learned

Teachers are constantly assessing—glancing over the room, eavesdropping, asking questions and taking stock of the answers. Based on all those microsoundings, I know that in those weeks archaeological thinking was alive in the classroom. Students were doing what archaeologists do, thinking like an archaeologist, talking "archaeologese," becoming engaged in the solving of genuine puzzles, and honing their skills of observation in a way that was relevant to their task. The students became excited and looked forward to what was going to happen next. When the teams made their conclusions, they wanted to know if they were "right." I would say, "You're right if you can explain all of your items. Remember justification." They would sigh, but go back to work. I'd just laugh with them. It didn't take long until they looked at the project for what it was—as a puzzle to be solved.

After seeing the videos of real archaeological finds—the Iceman, and the Inca Mummy—students remarked about the similarities to what they experienced. They could also identify how the archaeologists solved the puzzles and could follow their reasoning. They were reassured, I think, to see how long it takes even professional archaeologists to learn everything there is to dig out of an artifact or a site.

More explicit assessment also went on constantly between me and the students. To keep the students on task in a timely manner, I gave them due dates for each section of the project. Given this shared tempo, each Friday we were able to discuss the different things we had learned during the week. Sometimes the discoveries were simple, such as where rice is grown in the United States, but even so, that information could provide important data for a team with rice grains in their find. Other times, our joint work was more complex. For example, as teams struggled to make more precise predictions about their finds, we jointly drew a Venn diagram on the similarities and differences among the Western tribes. I toyed with the idea of writing down our weekly responses, but the students seemed to like the open discussion forum, so I discarded the writing activity. What really made me feel that the work in progress was worthwhile was when one group inadvertently discovered something that would help another group and spontaneously shared it with them.

The evidence for whether individual students met the performance standard was embedded in the culminating activity of the archaeologist's report. From the outset of the project, students knew that the major criteria for their reports were these:

- Every item from the Find must be accounted for and explained.
- All statements concerning the tribe and biome must be backed up with evidence.
- The report should give evidence that you have learned to think like an archaeologist, specifically that you can put the scientific method of investigation to good use.
- The final report has to be written as if it were ready to be published. It must be typed and checked carefully for grammar, spelling, and so on.

In addition to individually written reports, each archaeological team also made a presentation about their find. The presentation was followed by a question-and-answer period at the end. I thought of this as providing me with still another assessment of what the class as a whole had learned. It was not necessarily an easy process, however. My students had not had much background in asking challenging questions. They started by asking things like "Which artifact was the most difficult for you to identify?" They would, I think, have stayed at that level, except that we paused and worked on developing better questions. To remind them of their responsibilities as interviewers, I wrote WHY? HOW? and BECAUSE in huge chalk letters on the board behind the presenters. Gradually, the questions became more along the lines of "How did you reach that conclusion?" and "What did you learn from this project?" Some progress, but we clearly had a ways to go.

Reflections: Next Time Around

Interdisciplinary units can be a powerful context for teaching thinking. Or they can waste the already limited time we have for learning. I have to ask myself constantly, "Does this project have the kind of integrity my students deserve?" I have to ask, "Would this stand *on its own* as good science?" And, I have to know that the science and the humanities I am teaching are stronger for being in conversation with one another. It is the difference in what chemists call a mixture and a compound. In the first, the molecules of one substance simply mix with those of the second ingredient. But in a compound, a chemical change takes place and a wholly new substance emerges. My sense is that we have this kind of compound in the archaeology unit. There students can learn how to investigate. And while they sharpen their inquiry and observation skills, they are using important mathematical operations and concepts, finding out how to read literature as an index of a people's worldview, and practicing both written and spoken argument.

But serious classroom teaching is exactly like a complex archaeological find. No sooner is one puzzle cleared up than another becomes apparent. So, yes, over the three years I have taught the Native American project, I have learned a good deal about designing interdisciplinary units with muscle. I have learned how to borrow the best of what other disciplines have to offer, such as the visual thinking skills of the arts or the computation skills of mathematics. But, in doing that, I have created a vigorous and demanding classroom environment where questioning, discussion, and testing ideas is a regular, not a sometimes, occurrence. To thrive in that educational ecology takes energy, organization, and follow-through. Students with learning difficulties or little experience with the intrinsic rewards of learning can get lost quickly. Students who couldn't skim and pick out relevant information, or who struggled to synthesize or infer, had a hard time. Students who were too impatient to engage in the Socratic seminar discussions just endured them.

So I am staring into the face of a new challenge. On the one hand, I have developed charts and techniques to help challenged students organize their thoughts. On the other hand, I am constantly watching to see that I'm not washing all the demand out of the curriculum. I have found that some of my students need a very sequential highway to the end product, with me checking their progress, encouraging them at each step along the way. Other students are in the fast lane. Some are on a frontage road or a narrow dirt path. I suppose that one way of thinking about it is to say that I want to create a very rare kind of educational biome—one where there are supports for those who need them and headroom for those who are ready to fly. It is an absolutely huge, and an absolutely necessary, assignment. No teacher should turn it down.

Response from a Colleague:
The Archaeology of an Interdisciplinary Unit

Jean Slattery

I was surprised when Dennie Wolf asked if I would respond to Lue Stilley's interdisciplinary unit on archaeology. Surprised only because I had expressed, on more than one occasion, my mounting disappointment with the stuff of which most interdisciplinary units are made. As a former high school chemistry teacher I resonated to Lue's early misgivings about teaching "one of those interdisciplinary mashes where all the subjects are shoehorned in and none is taught with integrity." So, almost against my better judgment, I agreed. And, as I read, fierce defender of "real science" that I am, I was intrigued, even compelled, to excavate the unit, analyzing its separate parts and appreciating its greater whole.

Lue is dead right: "Serious classroom teaching is exactly like a complex archaeologic find." And I might add, so is her thoughtful, carefully constructed unit. In gradually making sense of their "find," Stilley's students experience four different, yet complementary, kinds of learning that I think are the essentials for any interdisciplinary unit worth its salt. They are as follows:

1. Strong content knowledge—ratio and proportion, measures of central tendency, radioactive carbon dating, the effects of various biomes on their inhabitants, adaptation, and the similarities and differences between representative Native American tribes and between Native Americans and other cultures.
2. Ample opportunities to practice the tools of the trade—observing, inferring, classifying, collecting, and analyzing data using grids, Venn diagrams, and graphs, reading and making maps, keeping a field journal, making accurate biological drawings, and utilizing a database to interpret findings.

3. Attention to communication and literacy—reading, writing, speaking, and listening—academic seed corn. She makes sure her students read text closely, participate in Socratic seminars, revise their writing, and formulate probing questions.
4. An insistence that students grasp each discipline's "big ideas." In this unit, formulas emerge from "basic, observed, regularities in the natural world." Students saw that new knowledge in science is generated by painstakingly piling clue upon clue and by checking wishful hypotheses against evidence from multiple sources. They at least began to see that the truth of primary text must be teased out since the period in which the piece was written, the intended audience, and the author's point of view all influence the ultimate message. They discussed the meaning of culture, trying to enter and understand it through its literature; and an understanding of the natural resources and climate that impinge upon it.

Still, Stilley confronts the nagging, "yes I taught it, but did they learn it?" question. There is ample evidence the answer in this instance is yes! One particularly compelling example occurred at the close of the unit. When challenged to defend their assigning their find to the Pomo peoples, rather than the Paiute (the "right" solution), one team of students not only held their ground, but further researched the finer distinctions between the two cultures in order to identify two new artifacts specific to the Paiute for inclusion in the next year's find. Eureka!

Underneath Stilley's account lies the subtext of her professional odyssey in becoming a more effective teacher. She shares, for example, her false start in trying to link the Civil War with battlefield medicine—an effort that made her appreciate "the danger of turning science into a sidebar for history," and more significantly, that for students to learn to investigate they need firsthand experience. She also wrestles constantly with the issue of how to provide sufficient scaffolding for students who struggle due to poverty or language barriers, without eliminating the intellectual demands. Having created graphic organizers to help students "see" patterns, she found they worked for some—but only some. Facing that partial success, she has a new hypothesis. Perhaps if other students would model their thinking, that might prove to be the greatest help.

At the end of my reading, I had two thoughts. First, if this were my unit, and frankly I found myself wanting to teach it, I would develop rubrics with the students for the required scientific report and the oral presentation. Knowing both the elements and the level of proficiency required for a task can help *all* students to produce higher quality work than they do left on their own. Such frank discussion of quality is one way to share the academic codes that middle-class students learn by osmosis—and which all too frequently are assumed rather than taught.

My second thought is this: Stilley and her students live in a city with a remarkable natural history museum, rich in exactly the kinds of finds that students have to simulate—never having seen the real thing. So where are the circulating samples of the real data and the junior curator to talk about them? Where are the funds for a trip to the museum's laboratory where students can see carbon dating occurring? Where is the afterschool program where Lue's students can turn their interest into a passion? A teacher like Lue Stilley can go a long way, but imagine what could happen if the museums, libraries, and universities saw themselves as schools.

4

Image and Word

Pushing for Deeper Literacy

Bill Amorosi and Susan Barahal

"Look at this drawing of Gollum, Mr. Amorosi!" a student said, holding out a portrait of the nefarious creature from Tolkien's *The Hobbit*. "Doesn't he look sneaky and slimy?" The student was not a born reader, but the drawing was unsolicited, and the long sinuous form showed a deep level of the student's understanding. It was Gollum—in only a few lines. I hung this drawing just as the student handed it to me, no caption, no annotation. Only months ago, a former student of mine, returning for a visit, was instantly drawn to the bulletin board. "Wow! Who did this Gollum? It's awesome!" He had read the book a year ago, but the image brought it all back.

For twenty years I have taught a unit on *The Hobbit*. The students read the novel chapter by chapter and turned up each day to hear me lecture on heroes, or to answer the questions I posed. It worked: students remembered Gollum a year later. Yet it wasn't an approach that harnessed the imagination and affection that the book clearly sparked. What could be done? The answer was there—hanging on my bulletin board. But it took me a while to realize what Gollum was saying.

It was 1998—the sixtieth anniversary of *The Hobbit's* publication. It's not a birthday on everyone's calendar, but it was making me think about the remarkable staying power of the novel. In the middle of my ruminations, I had a conversation with Dennie Wolf, the director of Project PACE (the teachers and researchers behind this book and the larger series it belongs to). In the middle of discussing literacy learning in middle school, I found myself talking about my passion for *The Hobbit* and my unhappiness with the completely predictable way I taught it. She listened for a while and then said, "So why not bring out a new edition? Your kids could research and write a new introduction, do illustrations, become graphic designers." There was Gollum practically waving to me.

The idea didn't fade driving home or overnight. My eighth graders were scheduled to read *The Hobbit* in March. I knew our building was blessed with a talented visual arts teacher, Susan Barahal. So why not? I went to Susan and talked to her about the kind of unsolicited enthusiasm I routinely get from my "freelance artists." We talked about how, if our intuitions were right, students would have to read the text more carefully in order to render visually rich images and vice versa. Students could research and understand the historical and mystical background of *The Hobbit*, weaving that into a foreword. They could look into Tolkien's life to create a short but telling back flap of the cover. Looking back, I know we harbored two other large hopes. If done well, this kind of cross-disciplinary collaboration could help students appreciate the complexities and interrelationships of the subjects they study. And last, but in no way least, I wondered if that kind of concentration on the text, coupled with having to develop an overall design for the book, might foster an understanding of the themes running through the novel. Tolkien published the novel in 1938, on what was by then clearly the eve of the violence and destruction of the Second World War. His reluctant hero, Bilbo Baggins, was a young adult hurled into choices and responsibilities by dark forces. As students chose which events deserved illustration and discussed what imagery would convey the mood of the book, what else could they come to understand? Would they be designing new understandings, as much as a new edition?

At last the day came. We introduced the project with great expectations. We explained to students that they would be reading the book with an eye toward revising the Ballantine edition of Tolkien's work. Their new edition would involve illustrations, graphic design, and research for a new foreword and an author biography. We also let them know that their work would be published in a book that middle school teachers would be buying and reading. We promised them time with a professional book illustrator. We also offered them a great degree of independence. Although there would be a great deal of preliminary organizing, we had no common prep time; when I (Bill) was scheduled to meet with the English language arts students, Susan was teaching other students in another wing of the building. Besides, there was a huge amount to accomplish. Students would have to work independently, seek out sources for themselves, and move independently from classroom to studio and back. As it turned out, this responsibility may have been the greatest bait, as well as the best background for reading *The Hobbit*.

We divided the students into small working groups. This system enabled the students to make their own choices, thus generating an intrinsically motivated group of learners. Even in the case of the highly skilled job of being an illustrator, each interested class member created an image based on his or her reading of *The Hobbit*. And from this sampling, we chose artists who demonstrated the combination of interest, understanding, and visual talents.

Student Independence: Freedom with Structure

Say the word "routine," and most people imagine some kind of repetitive drudgery. But those kinds of regular structures can also provide the supports and the mutual expectations that enable learning and enhance collaborative efforts. First, in language arts class, the students would read the book in a way that would focus their attention on the creation of a new edition of the book with all the research and illustration a sixtieth anniversary edition deserved. They were to finish the book within a month, reading chunks of four to five chapters per week, and during this first month, each student would also complete chapter summaries to which they could refer during the building of the various elements of the new edition. In addition, students kept track of the development of the personality of the story's main character, the hobbit, Bilbo Baggins, on tracking sheets designed for this purpose. To further their understanding, they hunted for suitable incidents within the text to illustrate, using graphic organizers on which to make structured notations regarding at least six such incidents.

The "Individual Work," coupled with what turned out to be very lively class discussions, produced a preliminary list of possible illustrations developed by a small group of students. This information was assembled from the graphic organizers that all the students had completed while reading the book (see Figure 4–1). As our conversation unfolded across the weeks, it was equally clear that all the students would be able to write an essay describing Bilbo Baggin's development across the many episodes of the novel. Looking at Matthew Smith's sample (in Figure 4–2), it is evident that the concentrated reading and research that students did, combined with their sense of having grown into independent workers, produced a strong sense for Tolkien's larger message. It was a message that they believed the novel's likely readers—young adolescents like themselves—would recognize and appreciate.

With all this individual work in hand, the class divided into smaller working groups. One group was to research and review illustrations from other volumes and to suggest places in *The Hobbit* that begged for illustration. A second group would research forewords from other books and to write one for our edition. A third group would research the content of the cover flaps and back covers of other volumes to create our cover flaps and back cover. (The resulting student work is presented in Figures 4–3 through 4–5.)

Because these groups needed to work independently but share a common schedule and vision, we turned to the notion of weekly assignment sheets. These were based on the previous week's accomplishments and mapped out reasonable expectations for the following week. The sheets allowed the different groups to work freely, and also supplied the structure that eighth graders need (and sometimes actually want). The students inserted these sheets, along with the completed assignments the sheets required, in chronological order. This was labeled "Group Work" (see Figure 4–6).

Small groups devoted a majority of class time during that initial month to research the specific sections of the new edition for which they were responsible. Groups simply reported to class and then went off to the library, at times leaving the classroom devoid of students. It was oddly lonely without them in the classroom. The group was then to examine this particular section as it appeared in many different books. Group members took notes on their findings and pooled their information. They then developed a format and produced their original writing. The group then provided specific reasons for their choices.

In this way, each of the sections of the new edition of *The Hobbit*—front and rear cover flaps, material for the back cover, and annotations

FIGURE 4–1. Selected illustration summaries.

The Hobbit: Selected Illustration Summaries

Chapter 3:
The entire story is centered around the adventure, and in chapter three, they showed the map of their route and the key to the secret door. We liked this idea because it would give people an idea of the layout of the land and intrigue people about the journey to come.

Chapter 4:
A good illustration for chapter four, would be Thorin and Company being captured by the goblins through the crack in the wall. This part of the book was when the group was caught in the thunderstorm and they needed to find shelter. Fili and Kili found a cave in which Bilbo awoke to see ponies going through a crack in the wall. Out came the goblins who took them to the Great Goblins. This scene would be good because you, the reader, can see what the goblins look like and how nasty and dangerous they are.

Chapter 5:
For chapter five a good illustration would be Gollum after figuring out that Bilbo has his magic ring. In this drawing, Gollum should have a horrified looking expression on this face, because he was just tricked by Bilbo. This would show the reader Gollum's appearance, and the tough obstacle Bilbo has to face, by himself and with the other group members.

Chapter 9:
The illustration our group picked for chapter nine is a dwarf being stuffed into a barrel by Bilbo. Basically, this drawing would have only the dwarf's hat visible as he was being stuffed into the barrel. We only see Bilbo's body, not his head. This would be the best possible illustration for chapter nine because it would show Bilbo taking charge.

FIGURE 4–2. Matthew's essay.

The Hobbit-Bilbo's Development
Matthew Smith

The character of Bilbo Baggins in *The Hobbit* developed greatly as his adventure unfolded. This development showed him becoming a more grown-up and independent person, or should I say hobbit, than earlier in the book when he was dependent on everyone else in the group he was traveling with. There were three stages in which Bilbo's development occurred: total dependence, important member of the group, and finally leader of the group. Each of these can be related to the life of a child.

At the beginning of the book, Bilbo was totally dependent on the other members of the group. The incident which I think illustrates this best is when Bilbo and his dwarf friends were captured by trolls. The dwarves had sent Bilbo as a spy to find out what was going on where they had seen a strange light. Almost immediately after discovering the trolls, Bilbo was caught and held captive. As you can imagine, the fact that Bilbo never came back disturbed the dwarves, so they set out in search of him. This caused them to be captured, and eventually the wizard, Gandalf had to save the entire group. The incident clearly shows how Bilbo was dependent on the other group members for help and guidance and how he could not take care of himself.

But, by the time the group had reached the forest of Mirkwood, Bilbo had finally begun to show some real independence. The point at which Bilbo showed the most independence and bravery was when the dwarves were captured by a group of giant spiders. This event was sort of the reverse of the incident with trolls. Here Bilbo had to come to the rescue of the dwarves. Using his sword and his ring of invisibility, Bilbo successfully lured the spiders away from the dwarves, then snuck back to rescue them. He did this all by himself without any help from anybody. This is when I feel he really became independent.

As time passed, Bilbo entered into the final stage of his development: becoming a leader. This stage began around the time after Smaug the dragon had been killed and the men of Esgaroth were try-

continued

FIGURE 4–3 (CONT.). Matthew's essay.

ing to get some of the dwarves' treasure. Thorin, who was the unofficial "leader" of the group that Bilbo was in, was a pretty unreasonable person when it came to sharing treasure. He refused to even talk with the army of men. Bilbo realized that without his intervention a battle would occur. So, using his own wisdom and judgment, he took the most valuable jewel in the treasure, the Arkenstone, and gave it to the men of Esgaroth to use as a bargaining chip. Though his efforts did not completely stop bloodshed from occurring, he helped to bring together the two groups who fought as allies against the goblins. In doing this act Bilbo left behind all traces of dependence and became an individual person.

This idea of development from dependence to independence is easy to relate to the similar development of our special edition's target audience: children 10 to 14 years of age. These children are going through much the same thing as Bilbo was going through throughout his development in the book. The idea of children growing up and maturing into adolescents is quite similar to the changes Bilbo was going through in the beginning of the book. As the children grow older, they will find themselves becoming less and less dependent on their parents for their needs. This mirrors Bilbo's development toward the middle of the story. Finally, these young adults will grow up and live their own lives, becoming independent citizens, much like Bilbo did in the latter part of the book. So, even though this book seems totally based on fantasy, it does have a human element mixed in as well.

The growth of Bilbo Baggins was a very interesting subplot of this story. In the fantasy world of dragons, wizards, and dwarves, this was one of the most truly human parts of the story. While children may not be able to relate to a group of strange adventurers searching for a lost treasure, they can surely relate to the story of a person becoming mature, having to make important decisions by himself, and finally breaking free and becoming an individual.

for the illustrations—was generated by students using a similar process:

- individual student research
- combining the results of the research
- student creation of a plan informed by the collective research
- student collaboration in writing a final draft
- student reflection on the entire process.

The last two groups were to work on annotations for the illustrations and creating the graphic elements that would unify the new edition.

FIGURE 4–3. Back cover flap text.

Back Cover Flap
Danny Churchill & J. R. Manoogian

On January 3, 1892, John Ronald Reuel Tolkien was born. He was born in Bloemfontein. He was the son of Arthur Reuel Tolkien and Mabel Suffied. Tolkien was one of the greatest writers ever.

Tolkien attended school in Oxford, where he published his first writings. In 1911, his first published writing appears in his school chronicle. It was a poem called *The Battle of the Eastern Fields*. From the time period of 1913 to 1938 Tolkien had 18 other writings published, including forewords, poems, chapters in encyclopedias, and introductory notes.

In 1930, Tolkien started writing *The Hobbit*. He abandoned it before it was finished. In 1936, a woman by the name of Susan Dagnull of Allen Publishing read the manuscript of *The Hobbit*. At her request he finished the book. *The Hobbit* was accepted for publishing and was published in the autumn of 1937. At the suggestion of Stanley Unwin, Tolkien began to write a sequel to *The Hobbit* called *The Lord of the Rings*. In 1949, *The Lord of the Rings* was finished. The first two volumes were published in 1954, and the third in 1955.

In 1973, one of the greatest authors of the century died. Tolkien was 81. His spirit is kept alive by his four children: John age 80, Michael age 77, Christopher age 74, and Priscilla age 64.

FIGURE 4–4. Back cover text.

Back Cover
Groups 4 and 5

"In a hole in the ground there lived a hobbit. Not a nasty, dirty, wet hole, filled with the ends of worms and an oozy smell nor yet a dry, bare, sandy hole with nothing in it to sit down on or to eat: it was a hobbit-hole, and that means comfort. . . . This hobbit was a very well-to-do hobbit and his name was Baggins."

Bilbo Baggins embarks on an adventure with the good wizard Gandalf and thirteen dwarves. Little does he know this journey will drastically change the way he looks at life.

FIGURE 4–5. Front cover flap text.

Front Cover Flap
Stephanie Bondi, Kerri Sanders, Caitlin Courtney

"O very well," said Thorin. "Long ago in my grandfather Thror's time our family was driven out of the far North . . . and came back . . . to this Mountain on the map. It had been discovered by . . . Thrain the Old. . . . They mined and they funneled and they . . . found a good deal of gold . . . and many jewels too. . . . My grandfather was king under the Mountain. . . . They built the merry town of Dale there in those days. . . . My grandfather's halls became full of armor and jewels and carvings and cups, and the toy-market of Dale was the wonder of the North. Undoubtedly that was what brought the dragon. Dragons steal gold and jewels. . . . They guard their plunder as long as they live (which is practically forever, unless they are killed), and never enjoy a brass ring of it. There was a most specially greedy, strong and wicked worm called Smaug. One day he flew . . . south . . . like a hurricane coming from the North . . . and destroyed . . . Dale. . . . He took all their wealth for himself . . . and piled it all up in a great heap . . . and sleeps on it for bed. . . . We still mean to get it back, and to bring our curses home to Smaug—if we can."

FIGURE 4–6. Group work assignments.

Hobbit Project Group Work

Group 1. Divide chapters 1-14 by person more or less equally. Each student should suggest 2 sections to illustrate, explain the details of the section, and give the details of their reasons for choosing it.

Group 2. Two people should plan and provide a rough version(s) of a design for chapter titles; two people should plan and provide a rough version(s) of a design for the first letter of each chapter, one should plan a page number logo(s) or design(s).

Group 3. The group should write a rough draft of the book's foreword. Each should draft written contributions to it, and these must be attached to this week's product.

Groups 4 and 5. Three people should write the rough draft of a front cover flap, three should write the rough draft of a rear cover flap; two should write the rough draft of a back cover. Each should draft written contributions to their part of the assignment, and these must be attached to this week's product.

The students liked this format. The "safety net" of prescribed activities and deadlines and the trust in their ability to work independently generated an extraordinary degree of enthusiasm for their work on the project. The weekly plans also enhanced the flexibility necessary for this first-time venture. In addition, they helped students to manage their time and to meet deadlines. This method enabled the students not only to create, but through collaboration and reflection, to understand and define for themselves the shape and purpose of each of the written sections of their new edition.

The dynamic of the group producing the foreword to the new edition serves as a good example of how the entire process unfolded. At the very outset, members decided to divide the work of examining the forewords of at least twenty books equally. In this way, each one of them looked at a minimum of four. They, along with all other groups, used structured assignment sheets designed by me (Bill) to record their find-ings. Corri, one of the group members, presented a summary of hers in this way:

> There are many reasons why an author writes a foreword in the beginning of a book. One reason is to explain why they wrote the book. A foreword also gives background information, so you understand a little better about what you're reading. Sometimes they give the mood of the book, like whether it's happy, sad, sus-penseful, or humorous. In one of the books I examined, it had the setting. In most of the books that I looked at, it told you what to expect. To sum it all up, forewords are very important to a book.

Individuals in the group then pooled their information, and using it as a guidepost, invented a plan for the foreword they were about to create. This plan is reflected best in the group's final reflection on its work, seen in Figure 4–7.

Ultimately, the following finished foreword emerged (see Figure 4–8).

Students as Artists: Merging Word and Image

We needed an equally careful process to develop the visual imagery for the new edition. To begin its work, the entire language arts class met after school to look at what was possible in book illustration. While stu-dents pored over numerous and diverse examples of actual book illus-trations, we discussed one of our major design challenges: Our illustra-tions were to be published in black-and-white, so all the nuances, all the mood, all the creatures of *The Hobbit* would have to be captured through line and contrast.

We continued to meet after school to look at and discuss the various opportunities that artists have to enliven a text—not only through illus-tration, but also through graphic design. Paging through the stacks of examples from art history and the equally long history of book illustra-tion, students were intrigued by the graphic motifs such as those often found surrounding chapter headings. One excited student said, "Some of these look just like the doodles I like to make, Ms. Barahal." We also looked at examples of how artists can embellish the first letter of the first word of a paragraph, or decorate chapter titles and page numbers.

FIGURE 4–7. Plan for the foreword.

Plan for the Foreword

There were five major parts to our foreword. These were the introduction and Bilbo's development, written by David Kushmerek; information about *The Elder Edda*, by Christine Imbrogno, information about *The Lord of the Rings*, by Matthew Smith, who the edition is aimed at, written by Corri Nelson, and the conclusion, by Stephen Mantia. We will tell you about each section and why we wrote what we did in each section.

The introduction explains that the foreword was written by students and tells what will be in the foreword. We included this because we thought it was important that readers know that the foreword was written by students, and we wanted to tell what to expect when reading the foreword.

We decided to include the section on *The Elder Edda* since it would be interesting and helpful to understand the book, its characters, and where Tolkien's ideas came from. Readers would probably like having some background information of the book that they are reading.

We wanted to put in the section describing *The Lord of the Rings* because the storyline of those books is closely related to the storyline of *The Hobbit*, and if readers like this book they will probably like *The Lord of the Rings*.

We included who the book was aimed at because the readers could understand it was not just for older kids and adults. It also tells what type of story it is.

The part on Bilbo's development explains how Bilbo is like the children who will be reading the book. We felt this was very important because, since the book aimed at children ages 10-14, we thought we should definitely tell how the development of Bilbo from dependence to independence sort of mirrors the development of a child.

We wrote the conclusion because it tells the reader what they can expect to read. The conclusion sums up everything said in the foreword, and gives a little parting note.

FIGURE 4–8. Finished foreword to *The Hobbit*.

The Hobbit Project—Foreword

David Kushmerek . . . . Introduction/Bilbo's development
Christine Imbrogno . . . . . . Information about *The Elder Edda*
Matthew Smith . . . . Information about *The Lord of the Rings*
Corri Nelson . . . . Who story is intended for
Stephen Mantia . . . . Conclusion

The Hobbit is a fictional story written by J. R. R. Tolkien. But it is not just a plain fictional story, for it contains many themes and near-to-human personalities. It is an exceptional story for any age, but this volume is a special edition for kids. It has illustrations and cover flaps made by kids, just as this foreword is also written by kids. In this foreword, we will tell you about some of the places where Tolkien got ideas for this story. We will also introduce you to the main character, Bilbo Baggins, and tell you about a set of books, called *The Lord of the Rings*, also written by J. R. R. Tolkien that continues the story of *The Hobbit*.

In order to write a story, you need ideas. J. R. R. Tolkien did not think up *The Hobbit* out of thin air. It took lots of research and imagination. Much of this book derives from the Scandinavian saga called *The Elder Edda*, and anthology of thirty-five books of myths, religion, history, and proverbs. These stories were written down in Iceland in about 1300 A.D.

All of the names of the major dwarves in *The Hobbit* come from six verses of *The Elder Edda*. A story in *The Elder Edda* called "Siegfried the Dragon Slayer" had much influence on Tolkien and *The Hobbit*. The story is that Siegfried slays Fafnir the dragon, and takes the treasure of the evil dwarf, Andvari. In Andvari's treasure are the "rings of gold." These rings play a central part in the Tolkien stories, *The Hobbit* and *The Lord of the Rings*.

As you read this story, you will find many similarities between *The Elder Edda* and *The Hobbit*, such as a dragon who is guarding a treasure, a magical golden ring with power and a deadly curse, and a talisman of invisibility. Also there is a wicked dwarf who possesses a ring and

continued

FIGURE 4–8 (CONT.). Finished foreword to *The Hobbit*.

goes mad because of it. As you can see, there was a good explanation of where the ideas from *The Hobbit* came from.

Though *The Hobbit* may seem like an epic in itself, it really is a sort of an introduction to an even bigger story. This story, as we mentioned earlier, is called *The Lord of the Rings* and is one of J. R. R. Tolkien's greatest works.

Since this is an introduction to *The Hobbit* and not an advertisement for Tolkien's other books, we will only briefly tell you of the story. *The Lord of the Rings* is a set of three books, *The Fellowship of the Ring*, *The Two Towers*, and *The Return of the King*, that begin about 60 years after the end of *The Hobbit*. They include many characters that you will be familiar with after reading this book, including Bilbo Baggins, Gandalf the Wizard, and many others. You will also meet many new characters, such as Frodo Baggins, Sam Gamgee, Aragorn, and so many more that you won't be able to keep track of them all.

So if after reading *The Hobbit* you find that you like J. R. R. Tolkien's work and would like to read more, we can think of no better story to read than *The Lord of the Rings*. It completes the tale begun in *The Hobbit* and is a fantastic set of books. *The Hobbit* is for everyone to read, enjoy, and understand. Children ages nine through fourteen will like this book because it is a fantasy created out of different myths and legends. Age is no boundary; everyone who enjoys reading fantasies can get lost in J. R. R. Tolkien's world. Each character has a different personality that will keep you entertained. Bilbo will take you away with his adventures and Gandalf will amaze you with his disappearing act.

But though this story is great for everyone, this edition is specially designed for children who want to read it, or who are going to have it read to them. One thing that makes this story very special in that sense is beyond the physical appearance of the book, but lays in what J. R. R. Tolkien originally wrote.

The main character, Bilbo Baggins, the hobbit himself, is at first a very plain fellow. He likes to eat, to lie back and relax, take nature-walks, and do many other pleasant things. But the special thing is that

continued

FIGURE 4–8 (CONT.). Finished foreword to *The Hobbit*.

> he does not stay like that. He grows more in character, sometimes because he is forced to, and other times because he gains more experience with life. This is very much the way a child develops. As a child grows, he learns more, sometimes through mistakes, sometimes with age. So if you compare this to the way Bilbo develops, you will find a very special relationship between the development of a fantasy book character and of a child.
>
> *The Hobbit* is an excellent fictional story for all ages. Bilbo Baggins undergoes a personality change from relying on everyone else to doing things for him, to taking care of himself and helping other people. The dwarves and Bilbo encounter trolls, goblins, giant spiders, wood elves, and dragons. This is a great story, and we hope you will enjoy it.

These decorations often encapsulate a central theme of the chapter. We studied a copy of an 1894 edition of *Aesop's Fables* that presented the students with rich examples of how an artist can infuse visual interest throughout the entire volume. For example, the frontispiece, table of contents, chapter titles—even the end of every chapter—were all decorated. The students were excited about the possibilities and said they were already getting ideas. One student burst out, "I'm going to draw flames in lots of places in that chapter called 'Fire and Water'." Having read *The Hobbit* so closely and with the visual possibilities in mind, the students' own imaginations were brimming with possibilities.

As our conversations progressed, we moved from discussing the look of the imagery, to thinking about its role in drawing readers into the world of Gollum and Bilbo. In particular, we examined how artists chose to illustrate events in a story, noting that the illustrations reflected literal references to the text but additional elements as well. The students could see how artists often infuse their own personalities into illustrations. We concluded that as long as the artist did not contradict the text, he or she could exercise enormous freedom of expression. "Oh, like with Gollum—he's hardly described at all," exclaimed one student.

Our second major design challenge was to pare down their initial nominations and focus on the "best" events to illustrate. It was with this in mind that we invited Ms. Susan Avashai, a professional book illustrator, to visit us at school. After all, a "real world" task such as the production of illustrations for a new edition of a book demands consultation with the "real world." Speaking frankly about her own choices and struggles, Avashai spent an hour with us in the darkened auditorium, with her huge and bright sketches and illustrations projected on the wall. Using these images, she guided the students through the many stages: obtaining a contract; conceiving themes and subjects; and producing the work.

Using her illustrations in a book, *The House on Wolenska Street*, she showed slides of a number of drafts for a single drawing. Some of these were came from her own initial imaginings, others from historical photographs of Russia in the 1900s; still others were influenced by the advice or demands of an editor. Our students were awestruck that even adults with professional positions have to do homework, meet deadlines, and sometimes make changes or compromises in order to meet someone else's expectations. Students noted that it was much the same method followed when producing a piece of writing: multiple drafts with outside feedback leading to a final product. One student's perspective on Ms. Avashai's visit is shown in Figure 4–9.

The idea was to leave visualization of climactic scenes to the mind's eye, causing the drawing to enhance, rather than control the reader's imagination. A good example of this is shown below in Corri's work (Figure 4–10). She illustrated the final stages in which the forces of evil capture the group with whom Bilbo Baggins is traveling; it is here that their last pony is about to be taken. And it is the capture of Bilbo and the rest of the group that occasions events forcing an independence of spirit to emerge in Mr. Baggins. Rather than illustrating a peak event, Corri depicted a scene that eventually leads to several demonstrations of Baggins' independence. In making this choice, Corri followed the subtle route which Ms. Avashai had suggested.

The student-artists divided themselves into groups. One group would illustrate key (though not climactic) events from the text. The other group would invent ways in which to tie the new edition together visually. The latter group of students was captivated by the background information concerning *The Hobbit*. They were particularly intrigued by the runic alphabet after studying Tolkien's runic inscriptions found at the beginning of the book. They decided that the use of runes through-

FIGURE 4–9. Danielle's artist/illustrator report. **117**

Artist/Illustrator Report
Danielle Arrigo

On March 10, an illustrator of children's books named Ms. Avashai came to visit our school. She came to give us hints and ideas on how to produce the illustrations for our version of *The Hobbit*. She showed us three main stages in creating illustrations for a book: getting inspiration and doing rough sketches, making a "dummy" copy of the book, and doing the final drawings.

Soon after she receives the manuscript from the author, she begins sketches for her drawings. First she reads the book to find places where illustrations would be appropriate. Then she sketches some ideas she has about what the picture should look like. Before drawing the actual picture, she gets live models to come in and act out the parts. This helps to give a realistic feel to her drawings. This method would probably not work in *The Hobbit*, because very few of the characters are human and we have to use our imagination to think of what they should look like.

After making sketches of the drawings, she creates a "dummy" copy of the book. The dummy helps to show where the pictures and text will be placed. The drawing she puts in the dummy are usually very similar to what the pictures in the published edition will look like. I think it would be a good idea to do a dummy for *The Hobbit* because it would help us see where the best places to put the pictures would be.

Finally, after the dummy is completed, she does the final drawings for the book. Before she does this, though, she sends her proposed drawings to the publisher to make sure they are okay. If they say that the drawings are good, she does the final copies of the drawings which will be published in the book. In all, she said it takes about 2-3 months from the time she begins the sketches to the time she does the finished drawings.

Though Ms. Avashai mostly told about how a real book is published, she also have us a few hints especially for our edition of *The Hobbit*. She said not to look at pictures from earlier editions of the book, because these images would interfere with our own imaginations. She also gave us this trade secret: "You don't want to limit the reader's imagination . . . to reduce the possibilities. You get to a situation where you come to a climax . . . I think the best thing is always to leave that. You can illustrate the steps coming up to that scene." With all this information given to us by a professional artist, I feel that we are more and better prepared to create our own illustrated book.

FIGURE 4–10. Corri's revised pony drawing.

out their revised edition of the book would give it just the ancient flavor they wanted. Their historical research and their visual work began to come together in an exciting way. Having learned about the rune sticks used by Celtic peoples to label important objects or sites, they decided that the outline form of the sticks would be an intriguing way to surround each chapter's title. Titles would be written in runic code inside rune sticks, and in Roman letters beneath them (see Figure 4-11).

One of the designers, Meghan, decided to embellish every page number. She chose to incorporate the page number into the design of a ring because the ring is so central to the story. Inscribed on her drawing of the ring are runic symbols that spell the word "page." Meghan wrote: "The ring relates to the text by being a part of Bilbo's quest for independence. This ring in the picture is the one like Bilbo wore to fend for himself and help other members of the group. I think without the ring it wouldn't have given him the courage that he had to conquer all the things that he did. That is why I wanted to include the ring in my illustration."

FIGURE 4–11. Runic page illustrations.

Meghan left an area above the design of the ring blank to accommodate the page numbers. As she saw it, this drawing would provide the "publisher" with a template to be printed on every page of the new edition. Her design choices also carefully echoed the rune motif: the group decided to place the ring page design on the upper right corner of each page (see Figure 4–11).

Students remembered looking at examples of illuminated manuscripts where the glorious capitals conveyed and synthesized the meaning of the chapter in the design of a single letter. Also, deep in their histories in seventh grade, I (Susan) had introduced them to the art of medieval illuminated manuscripts, and they had created their own. (For a visual arts teacher this evidence of continuity was very rewarding.) The examples in Figure 4–11 from Chapter 8, entitled "Flies and Spiders," and from Chapter 14, "Fire and Water," speak for themselves—even medieval monks might not be disappointed.

Meanwhile, the illustrators were sketching away. It was important for me to keep them focused on the author's words, and yet simultaneously encourage flair and personality. As a former jeweler, I am a firm believer in craft. As a result, I discussed and demonstrated many possible techniques that students could use to make their black-and-white drawings fully expressive. So when they weren't hard at work on the dwarves' bodies or Bilbo's face, they were often crosshatching, stippling, and creating linear patterns. We kept up our looking, too.

As work progressed, we moved on from pure technique to talking about how artists use those techniques to convey mood and grab the viewer's attention. Line, shading, and composition were almost like members of the class. The students kept sketching and revising until they were happy (enough) with their composition. Then I met with Susan Avashai for a consultation and critique of each. Ms. Avashai wrote a personalized note to each student. For instance: "Corri, Make your opening for the pony smaller—or pony larger so it really is a tight squeeze. Otherwise this looks nice—good handling of rocks and planes. Go to town with the textures!"

Her notes urged students to remain true to the text, being careful not to contradict it. For instance, Tolkien says that "He was Gollum—as dark as darkness, except for two big round pale eyes in his thin face." But Jay's drawing of Gollum depicts the creature with slanted eyes

FIGURE 4–12. Gollum in the boat.

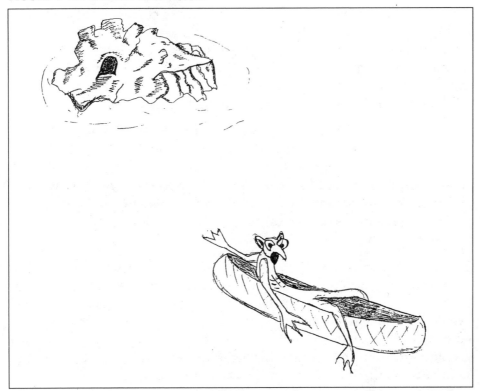

rather than big, round eyes because Jay said that he wanted Gollum to "look evil like the devil." Reminded of the text, Jay revised his drawing to depict Gollum squinting but with eyes that retained their roundness.

At the same time, Avashai's notes and all our work on craft didn't seem to dampen personal style. Jay also added his personal interpretation of the text to his drawing. He drew Gollum wearing shorts so that he would appear "neat." He also showed Gollum holding a bone to make him look "more viscous" and gave the creature muscles to make him "look strong." Jay carefully positioned Gollum in the foreground of the picture plane in order to show these choices. As Jay said, "That's how I saw him—as a savage."

Proof of this strong individuality, Mike presents us with a different interpretation of Gollum (see Figure 4–12). The drawing is powerful in its minimalism: it is the pure essence of the character. The Gollum of the novel is surely an evil and wretched character, and yet Mike's drawing conveys a vulnerability that elicits our sense of compassion. Gollum is evil but we feel sorry for him.

The illustrators, just as the graphic designers, were intrigued by mysterious and powerful symbolism of the novel. And they were determined to get it down on paper. For example, Danny's drawing depicted the precious treasure—the Arkenstone. Danny wrote:

> I think the Arkenstone is the most important part of the story because that was what the journey was all about. The picture I drew leads up to the whole end of the book because the conclusion revolves around the possession of the Arkenstone. I show its importance by having Smaug the dragon protecting and guarding it by having his arm around it. I also included other treasures like coins, rings and necklaces scattered around.

To convey his understanding, Danny drew the Arkenstone very large to emphasize its importance, but then had difficulty conveying its intrinsic brilliance, especially since he was limited to only black and white. We decided to leave the center of the stone white, but to include shaded bands that emanate from the center—bands that grow darker as they go outward from the center. This technique simulated the brilliance of light and reflective quality that Danny wanted to achieve.

This same concern for merging technique and message appeared in David's illustration of the rocky landscape that Bilbo and the dwarves explore while searching for the secret door. Tolkien describes the landscape as mountainous and, "if the map was true, somewhere high above the cliff at the valley's head must stand the secret door." Tolkien describes Bilbo and the dwarves walking on a "narrow track" and "at last to a still narrower ledge." They are at the top of a cliff "silently, clinging to the rocky wall on their right . . . in single file along the ledge . . ."

As much as David wanted to illustrate this scene, he had difficulty drawing the various planes in order to accurately convey the spatial perspective. He could not translate Tolkien's text to a drawing that satisfied him.

But then one day David rushed to my room excitedly and announced, "I think I'm getting it. I think I'm getting the perspective. I construct these buildings and things with Legos all the time and I thought of building the scene from *The Hobbit* that I'm trying to draw. I'm better with 3-D stuff. So, I put something together and it looks right. Do you think that's crazy?"

"Crazy?" I said, "I think it's brilliant! You constructed a model for yourself. You visually reconstructed Tolkien's text in three dimensions. This will help your drawing immensely because now you can more easily 'see' the different planes and levels. What a wonderful idea!"

Perhaps the most difficult aspect of the illustrations was the work of implying action—the "leading up to a climax" quality that Susan Avashai urged students to go for. Corri wrestled with this issue. In the text, Tolkien describes this scene as one in which the ponies "squeeze" through a crevice. At first, Corri drew the crevice too wide, leaving a lot of space on either side of the pony. This image did not agree with Tolkien's verb choice. Corri needed to comply with the text and to make the pony appear to be "squeezing" through the opening. Her revised version did the trick; the pony appears to have just enough room to "squeeze" by (see Figure 4–10). Corri also added a lot of her own interpretation to her drawing. The walls of the cave were not described in the book and Corri said, "I added texture to make it look more realistic. I also added some rocks on the cave's floor and a small spider to make it look creepy. It was just how I thought the cave looked. I got it from my imagination." She continued, "I chose this scene because it was an important part of the book making their journey tougher than expected." She positioned the pony to be the focal point of her drawing because of its importance.

Scott's drawing was also an effort to capture characters in action (see Figure 4–13). His drawing showed Bilbo stuffing the dwarves into the barrels in order for them to escape down the river: "The reason I chose this scene was to add humor to a serious situation." Scott left much to the viewer's imagination, not showing much of Bilbo other than his hairy toes. Scott also allowed us to imagine just how Bilbo gets the dwarves into the barrels, by depicting the scene as Bilbo pushes the lid down on the dwarves. Not much is drawn of the dwarf except for the top of his hat. In his illustration, Scott captured the meaning of Tolkien's passage, and dramatized the event with both humor and empathy. He transmitted the action to the viewer, and conveyed the importance of Bilbo's character by portraying him at a physically higher level than the

FIGURE 4–13. Scott's drawing of Bilbo stuffing the dwarves in barrels.

dwarves and ourselves.

As work continued, the students went from being solo artists to working together as if the classroom had become a design studio. As the students drew, an overriding theme of independence continually emerged, just as it had in text. Gradually, each illustration, though

FIGURE 4–14. Katie's key and map illustration.

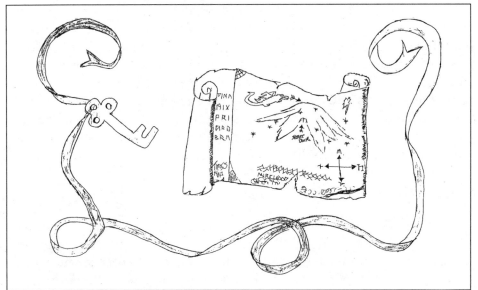

unique in style, came to echo and reinforce this theme. The merging of the graphic design and illustrations first showed up in Katie's work (Figure 4–14). She chose to draw the key and map because, as she put it, "without them they could not complete the mission. I didn't consider drawing anything else because this is very important. It relates to the whole book because it is the mission and without it they may have been killed. I put the ribbon in because it shows how close and important the key is to them."

She decided to enlarge the key and thread a ribbon through it in order to balance the composition visually. In doing so, she also referred to the text, since Thorin wore the key around his neck: "I added the ribbon on the key to show that they had to have it close to them at all times, around the neck or around the belt." Here were drawings that could be used to link the ring and rune stick themes to the illustrations of climactic events.

In part, this coming together was stimulated by the Review Boards we created. After drawings had gone through several drafts, the class was divided into two main groups: student-artists and student-interviewers. At the suggestion of a group of students whose task it was to structure the Review Boards, the large group of interviewers was divided into several smaller units. One student, Peter, set up the details of the plan in this way: "We could have three different stations around the room for interviewing. At each station there will be two people. One is the interviewer, who will ask the questions, and the other is the recorder, who will record the answers. After this process, we will discuss the answers and come to some conclusions." The Review Boards were designed to prompt the artists to reflect on several issues related to their work. We used a set of questions for illustrators and another for the designers (Figure 4–15).

Reflection

As eighth graders, our students are both joyfully and painfully aware of the extent to which they are and must be dependent upon their parents and teachers. They struggle daily with their desire to become fully independent and self-reliant. Bilbo's character is someone with whom these students can identify. His adventures force him to be resourceful, take risks, assume responsibilities, make independent decisions, and meet high expectations. This year's group of students quite unanimously and passionately embraced the theme. The following excerpt is taken from our student-written foreword:

> The main character, Bilbo Baggins, the hobbit himself, is at first a
> very plain fellow. He likes to eat, to lie back and relax, take
> nature-walks, and do many other pleasant things. But the special
> thing is that he does not stay like that. He grows more in charac-
> ter, sometimes because he is forced to, and other times because he
> gains more experience with life. This is very much the way a child
> develops. As a child grows, he learns more, sometimes through
> mistakes, sometimes with age. So if you compare this to the way
> Bilbo develops, you will find a very special relationship between
> the development of a fantasy book character and of a child.

Throughout this project, we both were struck by how seriously our students approached their work. They were highly motivated and worked independently to meet deadlines with a sense of purpose. They completed numerous tasks and revised without questioning or complaint.

FIGURE 4–15. Questions for illustrators and designers.

Illustrators: Questions to consider when choosing scenes to illustrate and places to decorate:

1. What made you choose this particular scene? Does it show an action or perhaps an event that leads up to a major event in the book?
2. What visual opportunities does this section of the story offer? Can you show landscapes, creatures, animals, costumes, interesting objects, dramatic or theatrical settings, or emotions?
3. What interpretations of the drawing are exactly from the reading? Why?
4. What additional touches will you add? How can you depart from the text and add your own personal and creative artistic statement?
5. How do you plan to show space and the point of view? Will the viewer be up close? Will there be a view of the distance? Give reasons for your decisions.
6. How do you plan to arrange your illustration? For example, where do you want the focal point to be? Why? How will you grab the viewer's attention and lead his/her eyes to the various parts of your illustration? How will you exploit the following: line, texture, unity, pattern, rhythm, movement, relative size, balance, space, drama, shape, value (highlights & shadows), emphasis, contrast?

Designers
1. Where do you want to include a decoration and why?
2. How does the appearance of the decoration relate to the text and its meaning?
3. What can you add that is a new idea (something that wasn't in the reading)?
4. Where will your illustration or decoration be placed on the page? Do you plan to incorporate the illustration with any text? What are the reasons for your decisions?

Like Bilbo, responsibilities and a sense of adventure were thrust upon them and they ran with it with enthusiasm. They seemed to like the idea of being admitted into the life of adulthood—of being able to rub elbows with a professional artist, take direction from an editor at Heinemann, and to have their ideas and opinions published in a book right alongside of Harvard researchers.

They experienced Bilbo's journey firsthand, if on paper. They gained the tools of independent learning. And perhaps ever after they will read with their mind's eye.

References

Ernst, Karen. 1994. *Picturing Learning.* Portsmouth, NH: Heinemann.

Hearne, Betsy. 1989. *Beauty and the Beast: Visions and Revisions of an Old Tale.* Chicago: University of Chicago Press.

Herman, Charlotte. 1990. *The House on Wolenska Street.* New York: E.P. Dutton.

Jacobs, Joseph. 1966. *The Fable of Aesop.* New York: Schocken Books.

Page, R. I. 1987. *Runes.* Berkeley: University of California Press.

Perkins, David. 1992. *Smart Schools.* New York: The Free Press.

Stevenson, Chris, and Judy Carr, eds. 1987. *Integrated Studies in the Middle Grades: "Dancing Through Walls."* New York: Teachers College Press.

Tolkien, J. R. R. 1982. *The Hobbit.* New York: Ballantine Books.

Response from a Colleague:
A Silent Partner Speaks

Conversation with Susan Avashai

In my work as an illustrator, I look forward to the opportunities I have to go into schools and talk with students about what I do. So I very much enjoyed being able to participate in *The Hobbit* project at Belmonte Middle School. When people imagine an illustrator, I am convinced they see someone leaning over a sketch pad, alone in a studio. But any book is a conversation between many partners. In this way, *The Hobbit* project was very authentic. Students had varied tasks: some were illustrators; some were writers who wrote the new foreword; others created the text for the cover flaps. Each informed the work of the others.

In presenting my work to the students, I used the case of a book I illustrated, *The House on Wolenska Street*. It is the story of a Jewish family in the early part of the twentieth century. It is true that the publisher bought it long before I was ever involved with the book. By the time I got it, the story was finished. But, whether I see them or not, the authors are always with me. Usually, an author has been as descriptive as possible with words. But where he or she has left cracks or blanks, it's for me to take over. The only thing I can't do is contradict the text, which would confuse the reader. But I can certainly contribute elements that were not mentioned. I have the power to elaborate. In this particular case, the story takes place in Russia in 1915. I researched the clothing people wore then, the houses in which they lived, the lanterns they used, and so on (I guess you could say they knew me well at my local library). Nevertheless, I remained grounded in what the author had given me.

Also, somewhere in my mind, other visual artists are always silent partners. I collect children's books based mainly on their illustrations.

There are some people who, I feel, are almost like my teachers. But for *The House on Wolenska Street,* I turned to photographs. I went to the Israeli bookstore in Brookline, Massachusetts, where they have a wide selection of photographs of that world before it was destroyed. I needed to see how people dressed and what that era "looked like." I spent the day there looking at books and felt, in fact, like I was living in that world.

Although I wasn't drawing on the specific work of other illustrators, I was working in a tradition that has been built by others. There are unwritten rules to be learned by looking at good artists' work. For example, one learns that it is important to pick moments that are highly visual. In other words, it is of little interest to illustrate someone in the process of thinking. An illustrator must take a moment of genuine action as portrayed in the text. Even then it cannot be the highest point of action because an illustrator would risk completing it for the reader. We don't want to do it all for them. Rather, we want to enhance the author's words. This rule helps me select the best moments in the text.

Additionally, illustrators don't want to cover too much. We want to find one moment that can help a reader along the way. In that respect, I suppose I often do the work of movie directors. I do so in determining how one line moves into the next, or how one scene becomes another. As illustrators, we sometimes want to be able to "zoom in" or perhaps approach the scene from above; we try to vary the angle. In that way, we are always assessing where would the "camera" be.

My family was really a partner in the book as well. First, my grandparents came from Russia and were raised in that era. When I was young, my grandmother had told me stories of her life there, and in that way I did have some background. It is my culture, so it doesn't feel foreign. Second, the backbone of the story is the relationship between a mother and her three daughters. Most of the adventures are adventures that could happen to any three sisters—something with which I am also familiar. I often use family or people I know to be my models.

For instance, there is one scene in the book in which the little girls are stopping off at a grocery store on the way home, and the grocer is fishing a herring out of a barrel. I set up the scene at home and used my husband as the grocer, and he was hamming it up. My daughters pretended that the herring stank. It was great fun re-creating the scene. In the end, I gave the grocer a potbelly and a long beard, where my husband doesn't have either one. I also gave him the right kind of skullcap and an apron—my additions to the character to make him appear authentic to the time and place.

I would have to say that my children are also coauthors in another way: I have learned how children read from watching them. For example, I learned from my own kids about detail. Take the classic children's story, *Good Night Moon,* where the illustrator included a little mouse on every page—a mouse that is never mentioned in the text. My daughter always wanted to find the mouse in each illustration. I realized that kids just love the little details they feel they are discovering. It may be one of the first ways in which children become readers. So I try to include elements in the story not mentioned in the text—things kids can find on their own—even in chapter books like *The House on Wolenska Street.*

Children outside my family have also been my silent partners in a surprising way. I've become convinced that we think anything that a child draws is sacred and that, as adults, we better not disturb it. So we take their finished drawings and we tack them up on the fridge. We don't want to ever come back and say, "Why don't you change this?" because we think we are going to hamper their experience. But we do it in writing and in other areas. When I work in schools, I deliberately show all the versions that any one drawing takes, and the corrections I must make. I want to show students that an artist has to come back and rework and edit visual work in the same way a writer does with written work. My work with kids has helped me understand that artists should teach the role of effort. A drawing is a work in progress for a very long time. Each time I mention to people that I am an artist, I get the response, "Aren't you lucky." So now I say "No, I worked at it."

5

Creating Companies of Learners

David Dik and Dennie Palmer Wolf

There is a dull hum in the classroom. Everyone is occupied, their heads bent over science fiction stories written by other members of the class. If you listen closely you can hear the slight scratch of pencils as students write notes and comments. Now and again, a student leans over to ask another a question. In every respect—visually, aurally, kinesthetically—there is every reason to believe that this is a moment of exactly the kind of teamwork and joint problem solving that every educational report and business roundtable calls for. Surveying the scene you would be tempted to say that here is a working studio, where young writers are working in the kind of collaborative back-and-forth of editors and publishers.

Or is it? Roam around the room and eavesdrop. After school take a look at the editors' comments: "Great Work." "Check your spelling." "You need more details." Ask a young author about this kind of peer editing, four out of five times she will grimace and say, "There are only two people who write science fiction well enough that I trust what they say and I only get them for a partner once in a while." Just where is the jostle and challenge, the push and the pull that is so often claimed for collaborative work? Under wraps. Beneath the surface. All too frequently, in the name of collaborative learning, we create exchanges that are fun, but doomed as learning experiences because they lack precisely the variety of perspectives, the depth of knowledge, and the motivations that flow through more genuine collaborations. In fact, more than occasionally, when we make the arts part of classroom experiences, we short-circuit the interactions that could inform and enliven learning.

Rather than creating genuine studios for learning where opinions are strong, points of view outspoken, and stakes are high, we practice wan simulations of the debates, rehearsals, and reviews that characterize the arts. More precisely, we substitute short-term sharing for sustained collaboration. We domesticate and corral interactions. We overstructure exchanges and dampen the risks of presenting or performing work to audiences. The loss is large—akin to substituting a harmonica for a French horn, a coloring book for a life drawing. And, more important, it is unnecessary. Using examples from a diverse set of classrooms we want to show that longer, franker, and riskier forms of collaboration are not only feasible, but vital.

Young Opera Companies: Deep-Enough Collaboration

The Metropolitan Opera Guild has a program, developed and refined over the past twenty years, that provides new insights into the social nature of excellence. The Creating Original Opera program provides training for teachers to form production companies, where students assume the roles of Production Manager, Stage Manager, Set Designer, Carpenter, Electrician, Costume Designer, Makeup Artist, Public Relations Person, Writer, Composer, and Performer. As a company, students develop a totally original work—working in a style that is authentic to the "industry." Each position in the company is interrelated and each task is codependent. The final performance thus becomes evidence of the work produced by the company—allowing the educator to see a progression of study that extends from ideas to design to building to performance. Because students are developing an original work from the ground up, the resulting opera projects typically run anywhere from several months to half a year. These more enduring projects, in contrast to shorter collaborations, produce much more than daily sharing. Under the best of circumstances (e.g., enough time, a teacher who is an alert and deft coach, and so on), the opera productions often foster a developing and deepening understanding.

For example, in Judy Bounton's classroom at Vroom School in Bayonne, New Jersey, students are writing an opera with a theme very close to their hearts. After several grades of open enrollment, their school becomes a selective school for the gifted. All of the students face taking the exam and the fears of not making the grade. Not surprisingly, in their opera, they invent a character, Charlie, who comes to Bayonne from Kansas. As a stranger from a different region, Charlie is not only an outsider, but completely unprepared for the headlong rush toward passing the entrance exam.

As students worked on their libretto across several months, Bounton helped them to develop a growing understanding of how they could use the idea of "coming from Kansas" to describe first Charlie's outsider status, then his plight, and finally, a longing for Kansas as a place where exams don't distort and harry the lives of young children. Samples from the classroom logbook of observations illustrate how the sustained nature of this collaboration fostered an evolving meaning for Kansas and a deepening understanding of how a libretto can communicate many levels of meaning.

> *Time 1*: Students decided that the new kid in their opera should come from "Kansas." They happened to have pen pals there (their teacher met a colleague who lives and works there) and for them, "Kansas" had the ring of being almost unimaginably far from their own urban environment.

> *Time 2*: As students worked on the libretto, the central event became the challenge and threat of gaining entrance to the magnet gifted program. To portray the arbitrary and harsh exam, the writers decided that the central character, Charlie, the new kid from Kansas, will fail the exam. He fails, not because he is lazy or dumb—but because he comes from a different place where people use language in a different way (saying "pop" for soda, "tennis shoes" for sneakers), and value different types of knowledge.

> *Time 3*: Once the basic tragedy was laid out, the writers began working on the actual lines and songs for the opera. At this juncture, they understood that they were also writing about the clash and mutual misunderstanding between two regional cultures. They began to make use of a rich array of cultural references (e.g., opera and *The Wizard of Oz*) to highlight and joke about this. For example, in a scene where a "city kid," D. J., first meets Charlie (they bump into one another while fishing), both are humming an aria from *The Barber of Seville*:

> D.J. : How do you know that song?
> CHARLIE: I saw the *Barber of Seville*. What do I look like?

D.J.: Hey, I was just asking. . . .
  (They talk over fishing, and D. J. explains that he fishes for eels, but does not eat them.)
D.J.: Want to take a shot at it?
Charlie *(Misunderstanding):* Do you have a gun?
(D. J. is disgusted.)
CHARLIE: I think I'm not in Kansas anymore.

Students wrote a subsequent scene where the city kids talk over the new kid from Kansas.

PAT: Where was he [D. J.]?
CHRIS: In the park—fishing—He was with that new kid.
CASEY: That little twerp?
JAMIE: Where is he from? Kansas?
CASEY: Candy-us?
JAMIE: Is that where they make candy?
CASEY: We CAN kids from Kansas!
(Charlie is nearby and he slams the tackle box shut!)
PAT: You don't even know anyone from Kansas!
CASEY: Dorothy . . . and the Scarecrow . . . Toto, too.
JAMIE: Lions and tigers and bears.
CASEY: And Charlie! He must be the Cowardly Lion!
CHARLIE *(Barging in):* You just better be quiet because you're talking about me and where I live. You think you're tough—well, you're not. Your town is no better than mine and you're no better than me! Why don't you judge me for who I am, and not where I live?

Time 5: This was the final writing of the last scene, where the writers were trying to grapple with the fact that they wanted to keep to their sad ending (Charlie fails the test and will not be going on the magnet program at "Liberty School." But he has made friends.) The teacher (JB) and the students talked about the final song, which is a reprise of an opening number about friendship—but this time they wanted it performed with a bittersweet twist. The students were searching for the name of the city in their opera. They wanted to make the allusion to Oz, because that would introduce the idea of characters getting what they really want. They hoped that the idea of Oz would help the audience understand that while Charlie is not in the magnet program, he has something much more valuable—his integrity and his friends. Here they worked on an equation between their own city and the Emerald City in Oz, where the Wizard gives people what they really want. The students and teacher talked over how they could alter the lyrics in the reprise to reflect all that has happened:

JB: I think the first part of the song can be a reprise, but the second part should be about what they are getting away from.

S: And now you can play baseball, even though you're not in Kansas.

S: You are in Emerald City now. Just like Dorothy finally got to Oz after all her terrible adventures with the witches.

JB: So what might Charlie find if he were in the Emerald City?

S: The scarecrow got a brain, the tinman got a heart.

JB: We can be pretty sneaky here. We still have the name of the town to choose. But Emerald City could be like hitting them over the head. What could we call it?

S: Jewel City.

S: Green City, we could get them to think Kansas, green city, emerald, lessons like in the Wizard of Oz.

(JB sings the lyrics of the opening song which is on the board.)

S: Why not just keep the rest of the song? Like at the beginning.

JB: We could.

S: No, it's different now, everything has happened.

S (*Speaking a line for the song, sung to Charlie*): You've found a place to replace Kansas.

Several specific features of collaboration, urged by the nature of opera work, stand out in this interaction. The students are authors, with the teacher acting as a coach, suggesting ideas, guiding the process. There is an unusual amount of attention paid to even small details such as the name they give to town. Students are well aware that even so minor a detail of the text is an opportunity for carrying out the messages and motives of the larger opera. But this was not the case early on in their discussions. Kansas began as an accident; it only acquired meaning over time—first by being tied to another work, *The Wizard of Oz*, and then by becoming the longed-for "home" that Charlie has lost and the counterbalance to the excluding and unfamiliar world of New Jersey with its cliques, clubs, and entrance exams. If this collaboration had lasted even three weeks, instead of three months, it is doubtful that "Kansas" would ever have been anything but the name of a faraway place.

Young Opera Companies: Serious-Enough Disagreement

But just because Creating Original Opera classrooms offer the chance for sustained collaboration does not guarantee the full-tilt of social exchange. A key part of artistic interaction is disagreement: moments when sharply different opinions go head-to-head, no holds barred. Extended projects, like the operas, certainly create fertile ground for strong beliefs to develop. But not infrequently—in the name of getting on with the process or avoiding conflict—these differences (which are in fact symptoms of a vigorous artistic climate) are papered over.

Teachers step in to make the decision. Peculiar forms of "fairness" come into play: "The writers got to choose last week, so this week the performers get to have their say." Or odd distortions of democracy crop up: "All right, the composers have three different melodies and they can't decide among themselves which one to use for the opening song, so they will each play theirs, and then we will vote." But when did majority rule become the best arbiter of artistic choice? Do we have to domesticate differences? Could different points of view be cultivated and allowed to simmer, could students have thoughtful but passionate discussions of alternatives?

The Vroom School's opera provides an example of such an alternative. As the writers finished the script, they brought their proposal for a climax and ending to the weekly company meeting. Charlie would fail the test, he would be separated from his friends, he would feel the sting of difference and shame. Several students—and their teacher—were reluctant. "It's too sad." "Nobody will like an opera that says bad things about the school, especially at the end of the year." "Then how can you have a big song with everyone on stage at the end, why would everybody come out for such a bad thing?" Other students were adamant. "It does happen. That's what the exam does to some people." "We spent the whole opera saying that he came from away and that he was different." "Lots of real operas are about even more sad things. People die and are killed."

The debate flourished. Writers buttonholed other students. They built their arguments and stuck to their guns. Bounton took up the other side: "I was nervous. It did seem too sad. And I admit that some part of me was nervous about an auditorium full of parents and teachers."

Two company meetings later, with the performance clock ticking, a decision had to be made. Remembering the discussion, one of the writers commented:

> We didn't want to give up. It's our lives, we know what happens. But some people still felt it was a bad ending. So we had to think that one out. We came back to the meeting and said we would use the same song as at the beginning. It's one where the kids sing about all the things they enjoy. So everyone can be on stage and so the end can tie up to the beginning. But it has a different meaning. Kind of sadder. Like Ms. Bounton says, "bittersweet."

Young Theatre Companies

For generations, students have turned in their work to the solo audience of their classroom teacher. But in the press for teamwork and collaboration, new frameworks and curriculum standards continually stress communication, whether the subject is literacy or mathematics. This is all well and good until you take a close look at this imperative as it translates to actual assignments.

Too often, students are at work for what turns out only to be a simulated audience. We ask them to write a letter to a friend commenting on the issue of school uniforms, or we ask them to write a paragraph to an imagined manufacturer, detailing what they found in their experiments with different brands of paper towels. But the fiction is thin, at best. If there is no one to be disgruntled or delighted, no one to request further data or challenge conclusions, what difference does it make to suppose that there is an audience somewhere out there?

In Fort Worth, Texas, teachers have formed an alternative school, the Applied Learning Academy, where much of the teaching and learning focuses on providing students with an opportunity to test their learning in the context of real-world applications, with real-world audiences, and adult partners. Several of the partnerships they have formed enroll students as active members of theatre companies. In looking at the life history of several of these theatre projects, it is clear that opera has no monopoly on using the social interactions characteristic of the arts to stimulate learning. In fact, these projects suggest several additional characteristics of strong companies of learners.

Young Theatre Companies: The Drive of Outside Audiences

As a part of their work in Texas history, ALA students became interested in the problem of how historical museums—usually packed and arid—might become more engaging. They decided to take a page from the practices of hands-on science museums. A sixth-grade classroom approached the director of a small museum in their community, the Cattleman's Museum, proposing to pilot a junior docents program, where students would study exhibits and design ways to extend and enliven them for visitors of all ages. As a first step, they wrote a proposal to revamp a boring and overstuffed exhibition about Texas ranching, which, in turn, they presented to the museum board who made the final decision. This is what they prepared:

A Junior Docents Project

Modifying the Tour for Younger Audience

INTRODUCTION
The junior docents who have been hired for your museum request to install an educational program which brings the museum to life. This will complement your interesting exhibits and get younger audiences involved.

TARGET AUDIENCE
The target audience for our presentation is children in grades 1-5. The reason we do not wish to do any group younger than first grade is because we think they will not be able to make the complex connections needed to comprehend our guided tour/play. We plan to practice with a group of third grade students from Alice Carson Applied Learning Center. The date we have set up for that rehearsal tour is January 4, 1994.

PLANS FOR CHANGE
We propose to weave a skit or play into our tour of the museum. The skit revolves around a rustler, his exploits, and his capture. Melissa goes first and plays Kerry, a regular farm girl. She begins her performance as part of the diorama and moves the children to the movie theater. After the movie, Jarreau, a bad rustler, introduces himself to the children and talks to them about his exploits. (Jarreau's character is talked about briefly in the film. The rustler, Jarreau, must leave quickly because he spots the brand inspectors coming.) The inspectors (Chad and Blake) tell a bit about their jobs and also about the manhunt for Jarreau's rustler character. [There follows a very detailed account of the episodes that take place to explain each of the different exhibits.]
    This presentation makes the whole museum interactive.

RESOURCES
We will need to use primary source materials from Memorial Hall and the museum's library as well as the computer software on cattle and the Texas Rangers or brand inspectors. We will provide our own costumes (with help from parents, friends, and teachers). We are planning to ask Justin Boots to help us with authentic boots.

CONCLUSION
Our group is very impressed with your exhibits as they are now and hope we can add to them! Thank you for allowing us to plan our tour and be creative. (Shambaugh 1995)

In the subsequent weeks, students used much of what they knew about theatre, museums, literature, and Texas history to create scripts in which live docents, costumed as ranch characters, wove together fact and fiction. They located costumes, and designed a brochure about the project to present to visitors at the end of each tour. As junior docents for the Cattleman's Museum, the students each performed an original first person narrative. They conducted a dry run with several second- and third-grade classrooms—without great success. The younger children fidgeted and wandered off. Perplexed, they videotaped their performances and the reactions of their young audience.

In watching the footage, the problems jumped out at them: the monologues were too long and crammed with detail that had historic but little dramatic importance. And in many cases the delivery was at the tempo of a speeding bullet, while the character stood almost stock-still. Students worked with a drama coach to develop their acting abilities. And they edited like demons: ripping out the overabundant detail, adding humor and moments of interaction with their audience. For example, here is one student's edited and enlivened introduction to the exhibit on branding:

Script for Joe Turner (An introduction to the brand room)
by Tiffany Turner

Hello there, my name is Josephine. They call me Joe for short. You know my great great grandfather Turner owned a large ranch. Can you guess how large? (Reply) Pretty big, almost all of south Texas. Yup, his ranch was perfect. He and his family hadn't a care in the world, until the rustling started. Most of his friends had at least one or two cows stolen. One of his friends had over 40 cows stolen; it put him clean out of business. Then one morning Turner got out of bed and went on the front porch. Can you guess what he saw? He saw something that he sure didn't want to see. As he looked off into the sunrise he noticed the cows were gone. Every last one of 'em! He knew there was trouble cause the cows had not been branded. Since the cows weren't branded he had no way of finding 'em.

You know most ranchers spend their whole life buying, selling, and raising cattle, and that is just what Turner had done. The main reason people started cattle rustlin' was for quick cash. Turner had never bothered to get a brand registered, which was very foolish.

He decided to go down to the county court house and registered his brand, the Running W. Can you guess which one is the Running W? The county clerk wrote it down in the Brand Book. The next step was where on the cow should he put his brand? Where would you put your brand? (Reply) That where Turner put his? This was also registered in the Brand Book. You know that branding is like putting your name down on a piece of paper. For years man has marked his property. Branding actually came from Mexico. Why men brand horses, saddles, and even guns. You know the same ranchers can have the same brand, but it has to be placed in another location of the cow's hide.

If Turner had had his cattle branded the Branding Inspector could probably have found 'em, cause he would check other ranches and at local auctions. Do you know what a Brand Inspector does? (Reply)

Well, Turner did buy some more cattle but this time he branded 'em.

I've learned from my great great grandfather Turner that when you start a ranch you first purchase you cattle, second and most important, GET 'EM BRANDED, so that if your cattle are rustled the Brand Inspector can go on an investigation and find 'em. Then you get your cattle back, the cattle rustler gets put in jail, and everyone is happy, except the cattle rustler.

History has taught me well, cause I'm startin' my own ranch and you can be sure I'm going to brand!

Thanks for lending an ear, and by the way if you see a fellow with dark skin, glasses and about 5 feet tall, it's been reported that he's been rustlin' cattle in these parts. (Turner, as quoted in Shambaugh 1995)

Students toured over twenty groups of elementary students, senior citizens, and international visitors. Following each performance, the team introduced itself to its audience, and presented each person with a brochure that described their school, the process students used to develop their presentation, and short biographies about each docent/actor. Following this initial phase, students met with still one more genuine audience: the staff of the Cattleman's Museum evaluated the program, using clearly defined standards that were negotiated between students, teachers, and the museum staff.

What students learned at the museum has become part of the working knowledge of the student body. Veterans of that process pass their savvy on to newcomers any time they are paired on a new project. The net result is a sharpening sense of what it takes to communicate information—and ideas—to others. For example, the following excerpt comes from an interview with four students who worked on a long-term partnership with Casa Manana, a nearby theatre that develops and performs works for children and families.

In this particular partnership, students are developing the educational materials that accompany the performances, including lobby and hallway displays designed to enhance the conversations between adults and children before and after performances as well as during intermission. Students are discussing the work they have done: designing and executing a series of panels that hung in the lobby and on the walls of the theatre during the run of *The Lion, the Witch, and the Wardrobe:*

INTERVIEWER: What is the point of having the illustrations there, why does the theatre want them?

STUDENT: Because sometimes the kids don't really grasp what is going on. Sometimes the story is complicated, like in this play the kids are moving back and forth between fantasy and reality and that can be hard to follow. Also, because since it's a round theatre you can't have a lot of scenery because you wouldn't be able to see what the actors were doing. So that means that a lot has to be suggested, not really there.

S: And this gives the kids a chance to visualize what the play is about and they can go around the theatre and say "Oh, we should watch for the White Witch to come out and to watch the snow melt and that kind of thing."

I: So, if I am a mother who is taking my little kids to the show how do I know to walk around and talk about them?

S: The first one is right there in the lobby and you would see other people doing it.

I: But I could know that they are there, but I might not know how to make good use of them. I might think they were just decoration.

S: Sometimes we have students there introducing them. And there are signs. But maybe we'll be writing questions to put up with them?

I: I see that you have several of them with the White Witch, why not just one for each character?

S: Because we weren't trying to show just who was who. We were trying to show what happens in the play, how the characters develop. So in the first one the Witch is smiling, just like she fooled the kids in the story. Later on, she has her arms crossed and she is painted in blue to show how icy and cold and calculating she really is.

Young Theatre Companies: The Jigsaw of Expertise

When you think about opera and theatre companies, you see that they are jigsaws of expertise: performers, directors, designers, and musicians each bring a specialty to the work of the larger whole. Compare that to classrooms where, typically, all or most of the students are working away at the same or very similar tasks. There are certainly going to be variations in skill, but there is rarely either deep or distinct expertise. In many respects, this means that the potential energy of collaboration is often never harnessed. "Wait," you may say, "what are the chances that any given middle school classroom is ever going to contain either deep or distinct expertise?" Unorganized and unplanned, there is little chance. But why not change those conditions? Why not develop classroom interactions so that they echo the distributed expertise of opera and theatre companies?

The students working on the Casa Manana projects provide glimpses of how this could happen. To begin, the students working on the panels each read the novel. Then they scoured libraries and video stores for every available version of *The Lion, the Witch and the Wardrobe*. Each one of them watched or looked at the illustrations in at least one version, bringing back both examples and appraisals of how the visuals either enhanced or detracted from the experience of the story. They also read the script and talked with the set designer about the production envisioned for Casa. Individual students each developed a sketch for several of the major characters. The group looked at those sketches, pulling the best features from each, and literally combined them on a single acetate transparency, which they projected on the wall and critiqued.

From that point forward, individuals or pairs of students developed panel-sized images. Sometimes, even at that juncture, the students depended on their distinct talents to achieve the images they wanted. For example, they were determined to create a panel that showed the Lion who had been drugged by the Witch, catching the pair just as she was about to do him in. But although they had a very clear image in mind, it proved quite a struggle:

> The first one looked like a cat that had been shaved and he was just lying down. So we decided to try and do another one from above. Because we thought we would be able to see the lion better and we were going to have all the kids leaning over it, but it didn't turn out right. It came out kind of silly looking. And the other one we had, that Nathan and Roy drew the table but they couldn't draw the cat, so we kind of had Ellen, she's really long and she kind of just lies on the floor, we had to kind of draw her in. But when we looked at it, we decided that it doesn't really tell a story, he's just lying there on the table, so right now I am drawing a new version of the witch and she has her hands over the lion and he is tied up and she's going to stab him.

As different students worked on different panels, they each came up with different ideas for portraying the complex messages from the novel. One student developed an image of the lamppost that the children first see when they emerge from the wardrobe into the kingdom of Narnia. As she explained:

> The lamppost is the first thing they walk out of the wardrobe and see. Every time they want to meet back to find where the wardrobe is, it's the lamppost they go for. And I came up with the idea of that as our little symbol, and so we drew it in every single panel. We thought that it is about the symbol of them following a light. It kind of symbolizes that this is in their imagination, and so every time they see the lamppost they know whether they are in reality or fantasy. Sort of like a compass for them.

A second student, with a different sense for the themes in the book, invented a different device: in each image he drew, he inserted either a vista, a picture, or a mirror reflection picturing Narnia in its green and garden state, before the White Witch destroyed it with her frost. Both of these distinctive devices, once developed, become part of a shared vocabulary for all of the panels.

But the most striking instance of distinctive roles only becomes visible once you observe the students at work. In this case, one of the students was in an earlier production of Pinocchio, and she had a sharp sense for the scale of the theatre and the need for costumes and sets (and consequently, the panels) to be bold and intelligible from long distances. Another student was clearly an accomplished reader who had a feeling for the symbolic and thematic elements of the novel. It was she who first picked up on the devices of the lamppost and the portraits of Narnia, and suggested that these images be used recurrently throughout the panels. She also urged the group to think about always painting the White Witch in icy blues and lavenders, and children in warm and rosy colors.

A pair of boys, who called themselves "the Disney guys," were accomplished cartoonists who supplied the gnarled figure of the Witches' dwarf wherever it was needed. They also provided thumbnail sketches to their peers who were struggling to draw figures in motion. In other words, in order to perform their assignment well, these students reinvented the idea of a company of specialists whose mosaic of talents come together.

Conclusion

In an overheard conversation, a chamber music player reflected on having recently played with a sterling string quartet, "They make me play better than I do." This is not a lapse of grammar or a moment of self-contradiction. Instead, he is reflecting on the ensemble nature of musical achievement. Supported and spurred by being one of five distinct voices in a larger whole, he has a sense of playing better than he ever would alone in a practice room. He is sketching exactly the kind of effects that peer interactions are meant to have in classrooms. But this vision of mutual invention and change is not the guaranteed result of asking students to pull their chairs together and "share their work." If anything, it will be the result of building companies of learners.

References

Shambaugh, K. 1995. "Jarreau Makes History: Whole-Class Projects as a Context for Individual Literacy." *Voices from the Middle* 2 (1): 19-22.

Response from a Colleague:
Hitting the Right Notes

Stephanie Urso Spina

People often think of the classical arts, and particularly opera, as inaccessible to the general public, let alone children. The Metropolitan Opera Guild's program is one of many current efforts by art institutions to reach out and build bridges across some of the many rivers that separate our society. It creates a world in which students freely cross boundaries that have artificially carved up the world into economic and social class-related divisions such as high and low art forms, popular and elite entertainment, as well as oppositionally ranked styles of dress, patterns of speech, and even ways of thinking.

In this program a classroom becomes reorganized as an opera/musical theatre company in order to create and produce an original musical work. An opera company classroom resonates with intensity of purpose, genuine curiosity, and the sheer enjoyment of the work that is learning. As a researcher who has spent hours in these classrooms, I always come away with the question, "Why?" So this is my chance to look at some of the underlying mechanisms and to ask "What makes it tick?"

I've known some of the answer for quite a while: interdisciplinary work, collaboration for a reason, a reason to go after quality, a rare combination of equity and challenge. But when I sat down to write this piece, a new understanding came to me. Most curricular approaches favor inductive and deductive modes of reasoning: the gathering of evidence to reach a conclusion or the working out of examples of a general principal. But what you see in opera classrooms fosters a third kind of reasoning, with a logic all its own. The American philosopher Charles Sanders Pierce (1839–1914) gave this reasoning a name of its own: abduction. Pierce uses the following examples of beans in a bag to

147

illustrate the differences between the three types of reasoning. His version of a deductive syllogism is:

All the beans in this bag are white.
This bean is from the bag.
This bean is most certainly white

The inductive version is:

This bean is from the bag.
This bean is white.
All (at least some?) of the beans in this bag are probably white.

But the abductive form would be:

This bean is white.
All the beans in this bag are white.
This bean is possibly from the bag.

Deduction allows you to make claims with certainty, once you are sure your premises are true. (It *proves* that something must be the case.) Induction allows you to test these observations through experience. (It shows that something *actually* is the case.) Abduction suggests that something *might* be the case. Like inductions, abductions start with an observation rather than an accepted claim. However, in the case of induction we start by assuming that we are observing certain facts relevant to verifying a *hypothesis.* In the case of abduction, we do not even know what the hypothesis is. Abduction is the process of making sense and finding alternatives that make better sense.

But here is what is key: abduction demands a constant (re)evaluating and examining the evidence from different viewpoints until we are satisfied that we have found the best explanation (or the best to date). This kind of striving for meaning making is what defines us as human beings. It is the type of thinking that will most likely be used by humans in any setting or situation that presents uncertainty or perplexity. Most of Sherlock Holmes' so-called deductions are really abductions. They are shrewd guesses or hypotheses based on keen observation and the ability to weave together disparate facts under a powerful, but tentative rule.

Opera classrooms are greenhouses for this kind of reasoning. Because students work collaboratively and because they are constantly in search of quality, what *might* be the case is at dead center. Just consider this excerpt in which a group of third graders are writing an opera about the arrival of a new kid in the city. The teacher (JB) and a group of student writers and actors discuss an argument in the script. The characters are about to vote whether one member of their club should be kicked out. The students look at pros and cons of it being a tie (2 to 2) vote or 3 to 1. The argument scene grows. They discuss issues of fairness and a number of alternative scenarios.

JB: If it's two against two—and I think we did this yesterday—we changed it from three against one?
STUDENTS: Yeah.
JB: If it's two against two, they're not . . .
STUDENT: It's a tie.
JB: It's a tie. So if Pat says "Two against two. We're throwing you out of the club." Everybody says . . .
STUDENT: Noooo.
STUDENT: I still think there's something wrong with that.
STUDENT: And why should he say that because if it's two against two you can't like isn't that like you throw her out . . .
JB: Oh. OK. Yeah. D. J., you're right. You're right. You're right. D. J. wants to throw her out.
STUDENT: D. J. That's me.
JB: Who wants to throw her out of the club?
STUDENT: D. J.'s sayin' that too.
OTHER STUDENTS: Nahah.
STUDENT: Who's sayin' that?
OTHER STUDENTS: Pat. Pat.
STUDENT: D. J. wants to throw her out too.
OTHER STUDENT: 'Cause he goes . . . That's how much they hate her 'cause he's gonna cheat his way to take her out . . .
STUDENT: Oh, yeah! I get it!
JB: OK. So maybe he doesn't say any of the numbers? He just says: "OK, we're gonna throw her out of the club."

STUDENTS: No.

OTHER STUDENT: Going to throw her out of the club. And that Pat says, "No. I am the leader of the club, you know, and I vote no." Then Chris is . . .

JB: The audience is going to see two hands for and two hands against, and D. J. tries to kind of . . .

STUDENT: Chris should say . . .

STUDENT: But it was a bad move right here.

JB: reads: "We're going to throw her out of the club." "But I'm the leader of the club and I vote no." "But it was a fair vote!"

STUDENT: Oh, yeah. Then he should be saying that.

JB: Who should be?

STUDENT: Pat.

JB: Pat's the leader of the club.

STUDENT: I know.

JB: And it wasn't a fair vote.

STUDENT: It wasn't?

JB: Well . . .

STUDENT: Two against two . . .

JB: Two against two. Does that mean you do or you don't?

STUDENT: Oh wait. I have an idea for it. When Casey comes in I think they should ask her: "Do you want to stay in the club or stay out?" Because it's even.

OTHER STUDENT: Yeah. And then the new kid could come and go in that club.

STUDENT: If she (Casey) goes out.

STILL ANOTHER STUDENT: I think we're getting off now . . .

JB: OK. But if she says she stays in that's kinda "There it goes. That's the end." D. J. has no reason to storm out now.

STUDENT: But she might say "I don't wanna stay with chickens, so I'll quit."

OTHER STUDENT: "I don't want to stay with brats!" "Yeah. I don't wanna . . ." "Yeah. So she has two reasons for it."

STUDENTS: Yeah.

STUDENTS: And she can say those little twerps or something like that.

OTHER STUDENT: Those little nuggets . . . *(Laughter)*

OTHER STUDENT: Those little Chicken McNuggets . . .
OTHER STUDENT: And they could . . .
OTHER STUDENT: Chicken McNugget. Chicken McNugget.
OTHER STUDENT: No. Nuggets. *(Giggles)*
TEACHER: While I am downstairs, I want you to iron this out. But I also want you to keep in mind that the opera isn't about this argument. This argument is just a way to get D. J. out of the park so he could meet the new kid. I mean this could be a Movie of the Week, this argument, but we just need it to be a way . . .
STUDENT: A way?
TEACHER: A way.

Notice the juxtapositions in brainstorming and the creative use of metaphor to lead to new insights. There is an attention to detail and a development of meaning by a (sometimes playful) process of association, trial and error, discovery and insight. The opera discussion is oriented toward the resolution of meaning through reasoning to the best explanation and it is not limited to any one way of reaching that goal.

To borrow an analogy from a philosophical friend of mine, Gary Shank, using abduction is a lot like learning to read another language. You don't have to give up your first language to read another one, but it will never look the same again. Using abduction does not eliminate induction and deduction. It is the thread that weaves them together into the fabric of deeper understanding.

In part because it is comprehensive and interpretive, abduction has often been considered a "skill" or "talent" rather than a "valid" and valued form of reasoning. But it is not a frill. It is at the core of creative thinking and scientific discovery. Abduction is at the heart of medical diagnoses. Any patient presents a group of symptoms (or frequently overlapping and misleading clues) and the search is for what could be causing them. A poet revising or a choreographer exploring alternative movements depend on their ability to turn over many possibilities, find the right one, and see the meaning of their work take on new dimensions. So abduction is actually our most important means for detection, diagnosis, and prediction. It deserves a place in school that reflects its importance in life.

References

Pierce, C. S. (1931–1958). *Collected Papers of Charles Sanders Pierce,* edited by C. Hartshorne and P. Weiss. Cambridge, MA: Harvard University Press.

Shank, G. 1987. "Abductive Strategies in Educational Research." *The American Journal of Semiotics* 5: 175-190.

6

Learning from Artists

Working with Teachers from Other Disciplines

Dana Balick

The central idea behind this volume is that understanding is rarely, if ever, a solo enterprise. Most serious projects, most inquiries and investigations, require moving from solitary acts to collaborating with others as equals.

My own experience as a contributor to the Moving Middle Schools series provides a good example. In Volumes 1 and 2 of this series, my name was listed on the cover as "with Dana Balick." That "with" acknowledged the fact that I managed the day-to-day logistics of the project, but it also pointed to the fact that I was essentially a silent contributor, never making public my own particular angle on the chapters that lived between the covers. But on the cover of Volume 3, the "with" disappeared. For that volume, I worked with teachers in the original discussions, read chapters, and provided feedback to authors. I went from assistant to engine. In writing this chapter, I am moving from engine to author. "With" has become an indispensable, collegial "and."

It is particularly gratifying to be contributing to a volume that has at its heart the important role that the arts play in teaching and learning. Over the past several years here at PACE, I have been fortunate to have worked on several exciting projects that clearly suggest the power of the arts to engage and excite students, and the almost magical ability the arts have to draw connections—connections between people, cultures, periods of history, and between learning and our actual, everyday lives. In all of the classrooms described in these chapters, the arts have helped teachers and students cross curricular boundaries that might otherwise have remained gated and locked. In the Jerusalem project, students crossed content boundaries to work with the perspectives of architecture, history, and current events. The students described in Chapter 2 worked to add literature, music, and dance together to better understand the Harlem Renaissance. In Chapter 4, we read about writers and illustrators working on a new edition of *The Hobbit;* we also read about companies of learners who work collaboratively to produce an opera or other serious work.

We have, over the course of working on such projects and compiling the stories that make up this book, realized another important truth: most classroom teachers are not trained in the arts. While it is true that many teachers tell of having taken piano lessons as children or singing in the chorus in junior high, their arts training more often than not stopped there. As they realize the value of the arts in their students' or children's lives, many of them find themselves wishing they had stuck with their music lessons, or had more opportunities to sing or perform as part of an ensemble. Teachers look forward to opportunities to bring artists into their classrooms, not only for their students' sake, but for their own enrichment as well.

Many of these opportunities to learn from artists come in the form of a quick fix—an afternoon workshop on book publishing, or a short, two-week residency with a storyteller or illustrator. Rare are the opportunities for teachers to engage in long-term relationships with artists or cultural institutions, or to become engaged in professional development opportunities that grow deeper and more sophisticated with the teacher's knowledge and experience.

This chapter will share examples of teachers working with other educators, all of whom are trained in the arts and humanities, all of whom rely on a wide set of cross-cutting skills that matter in their everyday work. These skills—noticing, inquiring, and exchanging—are the keys to being able to combine their roles as educators, performers, artists, designers, and so on. This chapter will focus on those occasions when teachers are able to shift gears to become learners themselves. If working and thinking across disciplines are so important, how do teachers acquire these skills for themselves? How do they learn to teach them? Since we have come to realize the power of the arts to urge real understanding, how do teachers with little or no arts training come to be able to use the arts, in powerful ways, in their classrooms? Specifically, where are there colleagues outside the classroom who can guide teachers as they gain the skills necessary to notice, inquire, and exchange?

What follows are three examples of professional development opportunities for teachers where the arts played a significant role, and where teachers were able to work with other kinds of practitioners over sustained periods of time. The first example comes from a summer institute where teachers spent a week working with a folklorist and exhibition designer as well as a Native American stone carver to learn how they could teach world history or culture to their own students more effectively. This seminar focused on the art of observation, of noticing, as the key to unlocking understanding; and borrowed from the disciplines of folklore, ethnography, and exhibition design. The second example is that of a folklorist who has taken the art and craft of interviewing, questioning, and listening into the classroom to model his techniques for eliciting stories with teachers and students. Finally we'll revisit Creating Original Opera, but this time we'll focus on the professional development opportunities the program creators have developed for teachers, which build over time and allow them first to become knowledgeable generalists and ultimately experts in a particular area of producing an opera.

Teaching Noticing: Working with a Museum Educator

Noticing is observation plus curiosity. It is what happens to looking and listening when you add in questions and the determination of wanting to understand. When I consider my own noticing skills, I realize that I owe much of their refinement to my mother and her lifelong love and curiosity about crafts and the people who create them. I have a mental image of the many titles that line my mother's book shelves—*Indian Baskets, The Spirit of Folk Art, Art/Artifact*—and find it interesting that for as many artifacts that line my mother's shelves, there is an even larger number of books. Her knowledge has come from looking and admiring, but also from reading, talking with artists, and visiting exhibitions. Likewise, in encouraging me, she has given me objects to look at, books to read, and has told me stories that bring the objects and their creators to life. This multifaceted appeal to my senses is how I have learned.

I brought this background along with me four years ago when Lynne Williamson, a folklorist and director of the Connecticut Cultural

Heritage Arts Program, and I worked with teachers in a seminar on world culture and history. We focused on *observation* as a way to research a people or culture, and then on designing exhibitions as a way to help others to notice.

To focus our seminar, Lynne and I chose to work with the life and art of the Haudenosaunee, a tribe of the Iroquois living in the region where our institute was taking place. Like the teacher-authors whom we have read about in earlier chapters, participants in this seminar immersed themselves in an experience that crossed curricular boundaries and relied on a wide array of research techniques—the core of which was observation.

Almost immediately, Lynne asked teachers to spend an entire half an hour with an object important to the Iroquois—a sweet grass basket. She literally asked us to *read* the basket as a way to enter into the Iroquois culture. We explored its size, shape, the materials out of which it was made—but we could only hypothesize about the basket's function, or its economic and aesthetic value. Out of context, it was difficult to learn much about either the basket or the Iroquois. This was our first lesson in the interdisciplinary nature of understanding. Without additional sources of information, our observations were oddly blind. Lynne intervened:

> Simply reading an object is difficult, because there is always going to be a lot of information which is not immediately conveyed from object to observer. Observing for information is a difficult and long-term process. It is almost a spiral where you work with an object for a while and then you go away and you do some other things, like reading around it, or talking to people about the object, and then you go back to it. You bring insight to it the second time that you didn't the first time. And then you backtrack and do a little more research. As you keep coming back, you gain almost a three-dimensional—even four-dimensional—sense of the object, because you are bringing more and more to your observation with each bit of added information.

But our lessons in noticing were just beginning. At Lynne's invitation, Tom Huff, a Native American stone carver, and member of the Seneca-Cayuga tribes in New York State, joined us. Tom, an accomplished

border-crosser himself, knew how many disciplines or ways of knowing it takes to *see,* rather than merely to look. In the brief time he was
with us, his stories and his carvings became our text.

On the morning of Tom's arrival, we entered our classroom to find a
tall man with long black hair pulled into a ponytail sitting quietly behind
a table covered with several sculptures. The carvings were white and
pink and black, with smooth rounded shapes. Some were literal, some
abstract—they appeared solid and cool like the stone they were born
from. We could identify some features of the work, the shape and color
of the stone, some animal and human forms, some landscapes. This much
was clear. But our observations became much richer, and more complex,
as Tom began to speak. He picked up a carving and explained that it told
the Iroquois creation myth—the story of the birth of good and evil.

Before life, we lived in the sky with the land forms. In the center
was a tree with blossoms of light called the Celestial Tree. The
earth was covered with water and was called the great cloud sea.
A couple lived in the sky world and the woman was pregnant.
Man dreamed of starting a new life, and was instructed to send the
woman down. The man uplifted the tree and the woman fell down
toward the great cloud sea. The animals in the water saw the sky
woman and wondered what to do. The geese caught sky woman
on their wings as she fell toward the great sky sea. As she came
closer, she needed earth to stand on. The great snapping turtle
agreed to hold up the earth. As she was on the turtle's back, sky
woman sent the duck to get mud from the bottom of the sea, but it
did not come back. She sent the beaver down, but it didn't come
back. She finally sent the muskrat, who brought the mud from the
bottom of the sea and placed it on the shell. Sky woman threw the
mud in all four directions and an island was formed. That is why
Turtle Island is the name the Iroquois call North America. Sky
woman had a daughter who mated with the west wind and
became pregnant. She was aware of two bodies inside of her—one
was born the natural way, the other burst from her left armpit
thereby killing the mother. Thus was the creation of good and evil.
They buried the mother and from her grave grew corn, beans, and
squash—the three sisters—the sustainers of life. Good and Evil

fought over their grandmother's body and during the fighting the grandmother's head came off and went into the sky which became the moon. That's why we call it "Grandmother Moon."

While Tom spoke, he turned the sculpture around so that each angle could provide a different piece of the story—Sky Woman on the turtle's back, the Celestial Tree emerging from the turtle shell, the beaver, the muskrat, and the duck. Our noticing, instead of being purely visual, became narrative. We could see the story.

Lynne explained:

In observing anything, no matter how young you are, or how basic your information or how skilled and academically aware you are, there are many things that come into play. One part is what your imagination will derive from an object. It can never just be between the object and the viewer. I think there has to be something else going on.

This was certainly true as we looked at Tom's carvings. The literal figures begged to tell a story that, until Tom began to speak, we could only guess at.

Having learned how much it takes to notice well, our next challenge was to think about how we could teach that kind of observation to others. To do this, we boarded a bus bound for the Albany State Museum, which features an exhibit on the indigenous people of New York State. Our challenge now was to explore how to make a culture—their objects and beliefs—apparent to someone who might know very little about the subject being portrayed.

At the museum, we immersed ourselves in noticing—observing with a purpose. As we arrived, we entered a replica of a Longhouse that featured a voice-over of a woman named Delia—a real person in fact, who told the Creation myth as visitors entered her "home"—a traditional Longhouse, which may have existed a hundred years ago. As we entered, Delia began to tell traditional Iroquois stories, beginning with the creation story, and the story of the "three sisters"—corn, beans, and squash. In observing the Longhouse, we felt like invited guests. Delia's voice, soft and welcoming, helped us to see the stories against the background of their beliefs, traditions, and opinions. Elsewhere in the

Longhouse, the figure of an elder was positioned in the midst of several other women and children who appear to be listening. Row after row of corn was tied to the roof of the Longhouse, animal skins dried above us. Lynne talked about this use of "museum theatre:"

> Here the viewer is inspired to bring something imaginative through his or her own observation—say through the senses. [This] gets the juices flowing in a different way. So that when you come to observe something else, you have a very open-minded way of looking at it.

Lynne adds:

> Delia's inviting voice made us feel like we had walked into her living room where her grandchildren had come over some Sunday evening and she was telling them a story. But it was hundreds of yeas ago, in fact. These elements of theatricality bring you into another world. They open you up. Without Delia's voice, the Longhouse would be dead. You would focus only on the artifacts. You wouldn't be thinking about entering the Iroquois world and having a greater understanding of their experiences. . . . It's all in the realm of imagination, but it's powerful.

At the close of the seminar, teachers designed their own exhibition on the Iroquois as an opportunity to explore how one would get others to notice. In the full-bodied ways they had learned from Lynne, participants constructed their own Longhouse out of twigs and branches gathered from the nearby woods. Tom's carvings were on display along with the sketches a teacher did as she listened to Tom tell the creation myth a few days earlier. Above the display, all along the perimeter of the room, another teacher had written out the creation myth. They had made a theatre for noticing.

Teaching Inquiry:
Working with a Folklorist and a Journalist

In Chapter 2, Karen Sorin asked her students, "What does it take to be known as an expert on a subject?" One astute student responded: "You've got to ask a lot of questions."

True. But questioning is an art more than a skill. Like dancing, it cannot be learned from a book. It takes a skilled teacher, one who makes his living by asking questions, to bring to life this important art. A few years ago in Wilmington, Delaware, two teachers were looking for a way to use their curriculum to address some big challenges at their school. For many years two different populations of students, those in a Spanish bilingual program, and those in the mainstream program had been polarized. These teachers decided to join forces and create a project whereby the two groups of students came together to write bilingual folktales. In order to make that happen, they needed a partner—someone whose own oral language skills would be a model for them and for their students. Greg Jenkins, a folklorist and then-director of the Delaware Folklife Program, was that partner.

As a folklorist, Greg's major tool is talk: the talk of asking questions and engaging people in conversation. In the folktales project, Greg worked with students over the course of a couple of weeks to coach them on the art of interviewing. Teachers were excited about the prospect of asking their students to go home and interview family or community members—especially since a primary goal of the project was to learn about people who came from a culture different from one's own. Students in the Spanish bilingual program represented a myriad of Latino communities—Puerto Rican, Colombian, Nicaraguan, Mexican—all of whom had parents, relatives, and friends with stories to tell about their cultures and the places they came from. The hope was that by bringing these personal stories into the classroom, students would gain an appreciation for and understanding of the kids they passed each day in the halls—but didn't know.

Working with Greg was an apprenticeship in questioning. He explains, "You have to ask a good question to get a good story. And you have to know enough about the person you're interviewing to know what to ask." (Again I think of Karen Sorin's astute student setting off on her exploration of the Harlem Renaissance.) He set up students to be "field researchers," who used interviews, conversations, and dialogue to collect information. These dialogues then became the raw material for their research and the basis for their folktales.

Greg loved the idea of teaching the difference between asking and questioning. He had spent years perfecting his own interviewing skills—sharing what he had learned with teachers and students was another way to explore his art. He did this by conducting "mock" interviews between artists and the students. One day he brought in a decoy carver from a rural Delaware community. As Greg modeled the interview process for students, he stopped as he went along to explain a question—why he had asked it in that way, and what information he was hoping to get. He explained,

> I think of interviewing as a wonderful exchange, as an art as well as a science, meaning that there are incredibly creative, dynamic things going on. I wanted students to begin to develop techniques for asking good questions. So we created working teams; one kid was the interviewer, another was the technician (holding the mike, working the recorder, and so forth), another student was a photographer—in this way they created an ethnographic team. Students had to bring in several questions they wanted to ask, but be able to revise them as they went along. The interviewer had to be able not only to ask the question, but to *listen* to the response and to follow up with another question that would provide even more depth. That may sound simple but in fact it is very challenging.
>
> At first, before having any practice, their questions were factual, such as "How long does it take you to carve that duck?" Or "How much do you sell them for?" A lot of them were questions that needed only "yes" or "no" as an answer, or the answer could be given in a word, like "Do you enjoy duck carving?" or "Are those ducks really expensive?"
>
> I talked with the kids about how these questions did not elicit any kind of detailed perspective about the *person* and/or his working process. Slowly they began to ask better questions. I also taught them a technique that I often use of bridging questions together like "If you enjoy doing this, why do you enjoy it and continue doing it." So what you are looking for are the "whys"— why someone does what she does. That was important, because as they got more depth in their questions the responses become more interesting and worth following with still more questions.

As we observed Greg at work in these mock interviews, we could see him encouraging students to see their interviews as conversations—an exchange of ideas and information. He explains:

Students could use their predesigned questions as a frame, but they had to allow for some freedom in the conversation based on a subject's response or particular interests. This often leads to wonderful surprises that you can't plan in advance. I think you can use this technique in any subject or in any situation. You can use it in science. I always want kids to understand that the method of inquiry requires you to create a way in which you progress through a conversation while developing an under-standing of whatever it is you're talking about. That is really profound. If students began to do this in more than just one pro-ject, if they did it six, seven, even ten projects throughout the year, they would come to understand that it's not just what information you get but it's the process behind it.

We kept stalking this business of inquiry. With a second group of teach-ers we found a second "interview teacher," this time a journalist, Lee Gutkind, who collaborated on *More than the Truth,* Volume 1 of this series. Lee, one of the founders of the field of creative nonfiction (or "immersion journalism" as he calls it) is a master of sitting down in a barbershop, a waiting room, or a diner and striking up a conversation that, inside of a quarter hour, is deep enough for an article, even a book. Lee led a group of teachers through a seminar designed to lay out the elements of writing powerful nonfiction. Right along with a reporter's spiral-topped notebook, chatting and asking were major tools. So was "finding a story." As teachers were sent out into the streets of Central Square, Cambridge, Lee offered: "Look around you. Ask. Listen. Find out." An hour later, one intrepid teacher found himself sitting with his guitar in a coffee shop, making conversation with a total stranger. By asking and listening, he learned how a person's life can slip, slowly and almost imperceptibly, from middle-class to living in a single room in the YWCA. Another teacher who interviewed a young clerk wrote: "I found my story in what the sign said was a 'revolutionary bookstore.' A few hours and many questions later, I left the store with a three-dollar signed copy of a book by Walter Dean Myers (of *Fast Sam, Cool Clyde,* and *Stuff* fame) and more important, my observations—the makings of a story of my own." For both of these teachers, the questions they asked of their impromptu interviewees supplied the fodder for their writing, as they tried to gain a particular angle on the complex, bustling, urban swath of Cambridge known as Central Square. Many of the teachers who worked with Lee in this seminar returned to their classrooms fueled with new techniques for getting their students to inquire by asking questions.

Based on her work with this kind of journalism, one teacher, Connie Russell Rodriguez, created an activism project called Making a Difference, which focused on Americans throughout history who had taken a stand on behalf of others. The unit culminated with students publishing a magazine discussing activism in their community and what it meant to be someone who took on the risks associated with making a difference. Interviewing and asking were at the center of this work, as she explains:

> We listened to an interview called "A Boy's Shelter for Street People" from a taped National Public Radio program. We wanted the students to think about asking good questions. . . . Students were able to hear how the interviewer's open-ended questions pushed the interaction along and made the story more complex.

After spending more time on the technique of interviewing, students generated the following list of what made a good interviewer:

A Good Interviewer
maintains eye contact
talks clearly
is observant
is friendly
shows interest
is curious
is flexible
asks good questions
looks for stories

Ultimately, her students produced a publication, which was a collection of reflections in the form of letters to the editor. Looking back, Connie commented:

> In many respects, for our students this kind of public writing will be critical for the well-being of their communities. But, in looking

over these reflections, what you see is how often an intensely personal experience turns out to be the key to understanding.

Connie took her experience working with Lee directly back to her students. Several months earlier, Lee had thrust her into an unknown. Likewise, her students emerged from an unknown with a new set of tools to describe, question, and persuade, and to understand.

Teaching Exchange: Working with the Opera

In the first phase of the Creating Original Opera professional development program, teachers spend a week of their summer as members of an opera company where they are the students, learning from a group of accomplished artists and performers who put them through the paces of creating their own original works. Under the tutelage of teaching artists like Shelley Bransford (of the Metropolitan Opera Guild), first-year teachers explore what it takes to write a libretto that will work for singers and engage an audience. Once they develop a theme and thesis for their "opera," it is time to come up with basic characters (without assigning names or gender).

One summer morning, I watched teachers work at developing the actions for their characters (still known only as A, B, C, and so forth):

TEACHER #1: A wouldn't say that. A is angry and self-interested.

TEACHER #2: But we need to make the point that A wants to remain where he is.

TEACHER #3: We don't know if A is male or female yet.

TEACHER #2: OK, stay where he or she is. The point is that A has a right to be there.

TEACHER #1: How about if A turns away from the group and rubs his or her forehead as though he or she is frustrated and doesn't want to participate in the conversation.

TEACHER #4: That works. A doesn't know how to express anger—A just goes silent with the rest of the family.

I felt like I was at a tennis match—the conversation volleying back and forth between people who were, even after a very short time, clearly invested in what they were doing. As they discussed personality traits and characteristics, Shelly vigilantly reminded them of their theme and of what traits each character had previously been assigned. In so doing, Shelly was modeling the kind of directing the teachers would later provide for their students. As the session went on under Shelly's watchful eye, they reworked and refined their ideas until their first draft was complete. The next day, teachers would work with a composer, the day after with a set designer. Then they would find themselves in a company meeting, exploring how all the pieces came together—or didn't. Having been a member of an impromptu company, and lived and breathed collaboration for a week, teachers went back to their classrooms armed with techniques to help their students do the same.

Under typical circumstances, the professional development likely would have stopped there. Teachers would be sent back to their classrooms armed with some strategies and some paperwork, charged with setting up an opera program and company and turning out a production sometime between September and May. But here it is different. Teachers in this program can choose to return the following year for Level Two training, followed by Level Three, and, as of this summer, Level Four—each one building on the one before, each offering increasingly sophisticated opportunities for teachers to hone the craft of *teaching*, or directing opera.

David Dik, Director of Education at the Metropolitan Opera Guild, explains,

> The goal of Level One is simple: to coach teachers in how to develop well-written, well-performed, and well-composed operas. The teaching artists act as models for teachers, who in this instance, are participating as students.
>
> In Level Two, we become more serious about the technical work (lighting, set design, and so on), and teachers become "teachers" for one another—directing one another's work in the areas of stage direction and musical direction. The artist takes on the role of coach. We build on what teachers did in Level One by using the operas they wrote the previous summer as a basis for discussion.
>
> In Level Three, the teacher becomes the full director—taking on not only the staging responsibilities, but thinking as a director when it comes to concept design and implementation.

The newly developed Level Four training will be a further departure from ho-hum professional development workshops, in that it will allow teachers to specialize in an area of interest, whether it be composition, writing, set design, or another of the several "jobs" their students choose in becoming part of their company.

This summer, an advanced cadre of teachers will come together to share success stories and work with real live set, costume or lighting designers, composers, actors—whomever will allow them to go back to school in September armed with new techniques to take their student-run opera companies to new levels. Not only will their students benefit, but teachers will continue to be challenged and engaged themselves—they will cross new boundaries in their own abilities—a rare and important chance.

Much has been written about extending the classroom walls for students, about bringing in outside visitors, going on field trips, or forming close ties to the myriad other institutions that exist in any community. But the same is true for teachers—they too need opportunities to learn from other kinds of experts, whether they be artists, historians, playwrights, folklorists, or others. And ideally, these opportunities would be sequential, offering teachers increasingly advanced skills, tools, or specialties on which to draw on in their teaching. So the next time you are given a chance to take piano lessons again, sing in a choir, or attend an advanced-level workshop, we hope you will remember these accounts and be inspired. Inspiration breeds inspiration, and surely you, as well as your students, will benefit.

Epilogue

Dana Balick

Four years ago, a small group of middle school teachers assembled in Cambridge to develop curriculum for their middle school students and to become part of a larger process of supporting one another's work along the way. Over the ensuing years, classroom teachers were joined by teachers from very different settings—museums, the field of folklore, and the rehearsal stage. What has resulted is a much wider discussion of teaching. Teachers have been a part of a collaborative process that has moved them from working alone to working with colleagues across the hall and across districts. The very process of producing this series has required that teachers share their work and their wisdom over time; and support a larger effort to prove that teaching, like any other demanding and creative enterprise, requires conversation, observation, critique, reflection, revision, and the ability to go back to the drawing board and do something again . . . and again.

That this volume on boundary crossing is the last in the series proves to be wonderfully apt. While these chapters tell the story of interdisciplinary projects, the entire series tells a story of how classroom teachers need and deserve opportunities to cross boundaries: into one another's classrooms, out into the community, and into situations where they can see other kinds of teachers at work—be they museum educators, folklorists, or a company of artists. We hope these accounts will prove useful to you as you guide your students across new boundaries, and as you discover the rewards of crossing them yourselves.

Contributors

Susan Avashai has illustrated many picture books and early chapter books, and has created the jackets for many novels. Her drawings and paintings have also been exhibited in galleries and shows all over the country. She has three children and lives in Newton, Massachusetts.

Bill Amorosi teaches eighth grade at Augustine J. Belmonte Middle School in Saugus, Massachusetts. Bill has been involved in the New Standards Project and Harvard PACE and is currently a lead teacher in the Massachusetts Performance Assessment Program.

Susan Barahal has been teaching studio art and art history in public schools for more than twenty-five years. She is involved in cross-disciplinary curriculum development projects programs and is a research assistant at Harvard PACE.

Larry Bauer is a principal of Solomon + Bauer architects Inc., a Boston area architectural firm specializing in institutional projects and working throughout the country. In thirty years of architectural experience with a variety of project types and clients; and in volunteer service on boards, committees, and his local historical commission, Bauer has had unique opportunities to struggle with the creation and preservation of "place" both as an architect and as a client.

Lynn Brown coteaches humanities to a cross-grade group of seventh and eighth grade students at the King Open School in Cambridge, Massachusetts, a public school founded on the principle of social justice. She wants to thank her coteacher, Julie, and her students for all they have taught her.

Julie Craven has been teaching for more than ten years. She has worked extensively on school restructuring and curriculum development programs, both as a teacher and as a researcher at PACE. She was coeditor of the first three books in the Moving Middle Schools series.

David Dik is the Director of Education at the Metropolitan Opera Guild. As the Guild's former Director of School Programs and the Program Director of the Creating Original Opera In-School Residency Program and Teacher

Training Program, Mr. Dik has developed and redefined curriculum and assessment strategies that are at the forefront of educational reform in the United States. Mr. Dik is a former music teacher and serves as an active clinician, choral conductor, and instructor throughout the world.

Robin Jensen is currently Director of Music for the New School of Orlando and is on the faculty of Rollins College. She is former Director of Education for the Orlando Opera Company and a former faculty member of the San Francisco Conservatory of Music and is on the board of directors for Opera for Youth.

Jean Slattery was a science teacher and administrator in the City School District, Rochester, New York, where she held the position of Supervising Director of Curriculum Development and Support from 1989 to 1997. She served as Site Coordinator for both the New Standards Project and PACE. Slattery is currently a visiting scholar at Harvard and working as an independent consultant.

Karen Sorin is the assistant director of a multiple intelligence shool, The New School of Orlando in Orlando, Florida. She has directed Shakespeare plays in intermediate and middle schools, coached chess in all elementary grades, and is currently teaching language arts in middle school.

Stephanie Urso Spina, a doctoral candidate in social psychology at the City University of New York, is an artist, a former K–12 teacher, and an instructor of graduate education courses in cognition, psychology, sociology, and interdisciplinary studies.

Luella Stilley teaches eighth grade life science and algebra at Memorial Academy for International Baccalaureate Preparation in San Diego, California. Ms Stilley is an avid writer of interdisciplinary curriculum and has presented her work at many local and national middle school conferences.